The St. Louis German Catholics

The St. Louis German Catholics

William Barnaby Faherty, S.J.

REEDY PRESS

St. Louis, Missouri

Distributed by University of Nebraska Press

Reedy Press
PO Box 5131, St. Louis, MO 63139, USA

This book is printed on acid-free paper. ∞

Library of Congress Cataloging-in-Publication Data: on file

ISBN: 0-9753180-0-4

For information on all Reedy Press publications
visit our Web site at http://www.reedypress.com.

Distributed by University of Nebraska Press
Designed by Nick Hoeing

Printed in Canada
04   05   06   07   08   9   8   7   6   5   4   3   2   1

This book made possible with the assistance of
Catholic Kolping Society of America (St. Louis Branch)

*Dedicated to my colleagues at the Midwest Jesuit Archives: Nancy Merz,
Mary Struckel, and Father William L. Mugan, S.J.*

Contents

✟ Preface

Since the true story of times past evokes wider interest than the imaginings of a writer, historical novelists today usually write true to time and place—but not always! Two well-known authors of recent books brought immigrants to St. Louis more than half a century before any group of Germans reached the midcontinent. According to one author, a contingent wanted to locate at the new trading post shortly after 1764. Sent packing by the French merchant-trader who founded the fur depot of St. Louis, these Germans settled a short distance south of the village the following year and began brewing beer. The other author tells of a prosperous German immigrant who made exquisite silver and lived in a three-story palatial brick home in the mid-1790s, forty years before any group of Germans, three-story homes, or skilled silversmiths found their way to St. Louis.

The truth may not be stranger than those fictions, but it is much more rewarding. The first German to come to St. Louis was not a brewer or a silversmith but a priest from the Rhineland, Father Bernard De Limpach of the Capuchin branch of the Franciscan Order. Spain ruled the Louisiana Territory at the time, and King Charles III had sent the Capuchins to Louisiana.

To prepare for the coming of their pastor in 1776, energetic Lieutenant Governor Francisco Cruzat urged the villagers to build a new church. When Father De Limpach reached St. Louis, he found the new building underway. He held services in the temporary log shed that had served the people as a place of worship. The church had the vestments and sacred vessels needed for divine service, even a monstrance for Benediction. Father Bernard carried that monstrance, bearing the Holy Eucharist for adoration in the popular devotion of the Corpus Christi procession each May. In May 1780, hostile upriver tribesmen, spurred by the British, threatened the village. They seemed awed by the pageantry of the Feast and held off their attack until the next day. Fortunately they were repulsed.

Early in the summer, Father Bernard blessed the new church, a structure of upright logs with a roof extending over the five-foot-wide porch, in the tradition of the French midcontinental building. The structure faced the Rue d'Eglise (Church Street), according to the plan set down by Pierre Laclede, the merchant-trader who founded the village.

The people then planned a two-story stone house as the rectory for the church. For twelve years, Father Bernard served the people well. "Father Bernard was much loved by his congregation," historian J. Thomas Scharf wrote in his *History of St. Louis, City and County*, "and traditions are still preserved of his piety and zeal."[1] Even though Scharf wrote almost a century after the priest left for Lower Louisiana, the historian may well have met older residents who remembered the Capuchin from their youth.

Father Bernard baptized 410 individuals of French ancestry, 106 of African, and 92 of Native American. Between May 1776 and November 1879, he solemnized 115 marriages of French couples, one of African, two of Native American, and one of mixed background, white and Native American. He buried 222 whites, 60 Africans, and 44 Native Americans. Spanish Lieutenant Governor Zenon Trudeau invited newcomers of various nationalities to settle in Missouri. Maryland Catholics of English or Irish ancestry crossed the Mississippi. As a result, King Charles IV sent an Irish priest, Father James Maxwell, to serve their spiritual needs.

In the record of baptisms, the first name of German background that appears is that of Joseph Eberlein, who was baptized on May 10, 1791. Joseph and Marie Rathe were his godparents. Marie Metz was baptized on June 1, 1800. Other Metzes appear in the baptismal records, but there are more Schulzes. From John Schulz, baptized on June 15, 1800, until 1840, forty-three Schulzes received baptism.[2]

Most of the early arriving Schulzes, not unexpectedly, married girls of French ancestry, including a Tesson from Florissant, a Valle from Ste. Genevieve, and a Menard from Kaskaskia. Other early baptisms of children of German immigrants were those of Sylvester Hab on May 24, 1816, John Leonstmetsker on June 20, 1819, and Rosalie Frey on March 19, 1820.

Henry Von Phul—son of William Von Phul, an immigrant from Westphalia—moved to St. Louis from Philadelphia where he was born. He married Rosalie Saugrain. The list of baptisms in St. Louis includes ten of their children.

In the meantime, Bishop Louis W. V. Du Bourg of Louisiana Territory chose to reside in St. Louis. His ambitious plans called for a cathedral of brick and a small academy for boys called St. Louis College. Among the one hundred pledgers for the new place of worship, eight had German surnames: Henry Von Phul, G. Brand, Henry Waddle, John Warner, J. A. Lichter, W. Risle, Joseph Klunk, and C. Wilt.[3]

Bishop Du Bourg stayed only a short time but brought many influential men and women with him: St. Philippine Duchesne with members of a newly formed congregation, the Religious of the Sacred Heart, from France, and Father Joseph Rosati with a team of Vincentian Fathers from Italy. With them, a seminarian, Franz Xavier Dahmen, C.M., came from the Rhineland. A veteran of Napoleon's campaign, Dahmen spoke French and German. Five years after his ordination, he began to serve the people of Ste. Genevieve.

In 1823 Bishop Du Bourg invited Belgian Jesuits under Father Charles Felix Van Quickenborne to open an Indian school in Florissant near St. Louis. Among these young Jesuits two would stand out: Peter Verhaegen, first president of Saint Louis University, and Peter John , world-famous missionary.

The steady, providential Father Rosati complemented the zealous but changeable Bishop Du Bourg, and he became his auxiliary bishop. When Du Bourg resigned his American post and returned to France, Rome divided the Louisiana Territory. Given his choice of New Orleans or St. Louis, Rosati became St. Louis's first bishop in 1827.

At the time, no priest in St. Louis spoke German. One was sorely needed. Fortunately, Father Joseph Anthony Lutz, a Baden-born but French-educated priest, had come to the United States in 1826 at the request of Father François Niel, the first priest ordained in St. Louis and founding president of St. Louis College. In the early 1830s, Father Lutz served the Cathedral parish as secretary to the bishop and acting pastor when the bishop was away.

Father Lutz celebrated Mass every Sunday for the German-speaking people, preaching to them in their native tongue. In the afternoon he taught catechism to the children, both in German and in English. Several of the Belgian Jesuits at Florissant, among them Fathers Charles Felix Van Quickenborne, Peter Verhaegen, and Judochus Van Assche, had some acquaintance with the German language, and Brother Henry Reiselman spoke German.

This was the religious situation in St. Louis when German immigrants began to come in numbers.

✝ Acknowledgments

Margaret H. Aylward
Matt H. Backer, Jr., M.D.
David Braun
Dr. Alice Brown, German St. Vincent Orphanage board member
Martin Duggan, editor emeritus
Martha Eise, librarian, *St. Louis Review*
Robert Frei, art glass expert
Robert and Marcella Garger
P. P. Hackett
Jean Henke
Noel Hollebeck, St. Louis Public Library
Jim Junker
Katherine LaForest (Mrs. Eugene)
Rev. Gerhardt Lehmkuhl, S.J.
Kevin Madden, journalist, *Labor Tribune*
Rev. Norman Muckerman, C.SS.R., missionary, writer
Rev. John H. Miller, C.S.C., Central Bureau
Tom Mulvihill, artist
Audrey Newcomer, St. Louis Archdiocesan Archives
Rev. Ralph Renner, S.J., consultant
Edward Rohde
Jim Rygelski, editor, *St. Louis Review*
M. Sallwasse
James J. Schild
Joan Short
Marilyn Steihart
George Sweeney
Mary Thien
William Vorbeck
John Waide, archivist, Saint Louis University
Ernest Winklemann
William Winter, St. Louis author

The St. Louis German Catholics

✟ *Chapter One*
Early German-Catholic Immigrants

How did Germans come to know about the area of St. Louis? Ten years after the battle of Waterloo (1815), Godfried Duden, a civil servant from Cologne, Germany, purchased land on the north bank of the Missouri River near the site of the present town of Dutzow in Warren (then Montgomery) County, about forty-five miles west of St. Louis. Land was fertile, abundant, and inexpensive, the climate moderate and of four seasons. Seeing a resemblance to the wine lands along the Rhine, he began to write home urging people to emigrate. In March 1827, he returned to Cologne and published his letters in a book, *Report on a Trip to the Western States of North America*. As a result, many Germans looked to the prospect of life in the area.

Overpopulation in Germany had spurred Duden in his call to mid-America. His fellow Rhinelanders had an added motive for looking to new homes overseas. In response to the presumed threat of French domination of the continent, the European powers put the Rhineland under Prussia. Avoiding Prussian military service gave many Germans, Catholics and others, an added reason for looking to America. *Catholics* from the Rhineland and Westphalia chose to settle in St. Louis. While Boston disdained "Papists"—as they called Catholics—and New York and Philadelphia merely tolerated them, St. Louis welcomed them. The French founders were traditionally Catholic. The Spanish regime (1770–1804) made Catholicism the established religion of the area. During the early American days, many Catholics from Ireland and Maryland came to the St. Louis area.

German immigrants began to come in significant numbers in the late 1830s. Westphalians and Hanoverians sailed from the port of Bremen and called their community north of St. Louis Bremen. Rhinelanders and Bavarians embarked from Le Havre in France and landed in New Orleans. The steamboat trip up the Mississippi was inexpensive. These Germans settled on the near Southside.

Records show that almost all of the German immigrants to St. Louis came from the three northwestern provinces, bordering on the Netherlands, repressed by Prussian rulers since the Treaty of 1815: the Rhineland, with Cologne its capital; Westphalia, with Munster its cathedral city; and Hanover, which included the port of Bremen. A few immigrants came from the mountains of Bavaria to the south, where King Ludwig I ruled. He and his people regularly helped the Church in St. Louis. The newcomers in 1830 found a community with 5,852 citizens of French, Irish, and Anglo-American ancestry, unlike their cousins who settled in Cincinnati and found an established Anglo-American city of 24,831.

By this time St. Louis had established itself as the economic center of the mid-continent. The French villages of Kaskaskia and Ste. Genevieve had declined in importance. Chicago had not yet come to be. St. Louis stood on a limestone terrace, free from floods, backed by fertile prairies to the west, and joined to the outside world by the great river, whose main tributaries funneled into it not far away. Geography made St. Louis the gateway to the West in the days of the steamboat.

Merchants and manufacturers in St. Louis supplied the farmers in Illinois and Missouri, the townspeople along the rivers, the travelers to the Far West, the trappers in the Rockies, the rivermen who plied the waters, and the soldiers of the western posts.

By 1840, the city had 16,469 inhabitants, at least half of whom were Catholic. Buildings stretched along the Mississippi River for sixteen blocks and went inland only eighteen. The census for that year listed workers in categories without reference to religion or ancestry: 13 were in tobacco, 15 in soapmaking, 26 in leatherwork, 28 in hat-making, 53 in the liquor business, 82 in printing and binding, 112 in milling, and 397 in building.[1]

By the 1840s, construction reached a thousand houses a year.[2] Most employees lived within walking distance of their work. Small shopkeepers lived above their shops. The fronts of houses stood flush with the sidewalk. An outside back stairs often led to the second floor. Among the builders were two immigrants, Francis Saler and Valentine Reis, who would take part in Catholic organizations later in the decade.

As the years moved on, skilled workers found jobs in some phase of manufacturing, as cobblers, brewers, woodworkers, wagonmakers, machinists, foundry workers, stone masons, mechanics, carpenters, saddlemakers, cigar makers, and wheelwrights. Some immigrants found work in brickmaking or bricklaying, and St. Louis soon won acclaim as a "brick city." By 1870, St. Louis was to rank next to New York and Philadelphia in industrial production.

Some with farming skills tilled "truck" farms near the city and brought their produce to the Soulard Market or the Northside Market to sell. Suburban farmers could travel the streets of St. Louis hawking their cabbages, tomatoes, and watermelons. More newcomers, who had been farmers in Europe, began to look to the rich acres near the French village of Florissant in the northwest section of St. Louis County. An early immigrant German was told by a friend in St. Louis to say to the first man you meet in Florissant: "Guten morgen, Herr Aubuchon."

The surprised villager responded, "How did you know my name was Aubuchon?"

It was a safe bet. A good percentage of the residents were Aubuchons. In fact, the newcomer's son would marry an Aubuchon.

Jean Henke, a descendant of three early arriving immigrants, tells of their coming from Hanover, Germany. Two brothers, John Bernard and Herman Henry Henke, led the way. They crossed the Atlantic on the *Diana* and took a steamboat from New Orleans to St. Louis. Farmers in Germany, they presumably had heard of the fertile acres of the Florissant Valley. They walked the thirty miles to Florissant from the St. Louis levee. The first of Jean Henke's Keeven ancestors, Heinrich, followed, as did another ancestor from Hanover, Henry Hoorman. Another son of Hanover, Bernard Knobbe, also chose Florissant. Other cousins of Jean Henke, the Degenharts, scattered throughout the district. Some settled in neighboring Illinois areas.

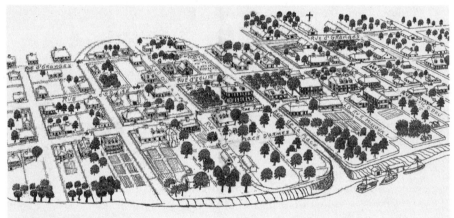

Above: St. Louis c. 1803.

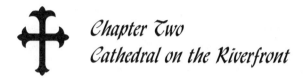

Chapter Two
Cathedral on the Riverfront

The brick cathedral built in 1818 had never matched Bishop Louis W.V. Du Bourg's enthusiastic praise. In 1832, Bishop Joseph Rosati called on the people of St. Louis to build a more satisfactory temple. Funds came in slowly. Still in Europe, Bishop Du Bourg, concerned about his former area, arranged a loan that set the building on its way. Finished in 1834, the building awed noblemen from Europe who had come west to hunt buffalo on the plains, as well as Catholic Iroquois who came from the Flathead villages of Montana to find a "Blackrobe."

In August 1835, Ferdinand Helias d'Huddeghem, a native of Ghent and a descendant of one of the distinguished families of Belgium, came to St. Louis. Father Helias, as people came to call him in Missouri, had worked for a time in Switzerland, where he learned German and held important positions. Even before Father Helias reported to his own Jesuit community, now at Saint Louis University on Ninth Street at Washington Avenue, Father Joseph Anthony Lutz met him at the levee and took him to Bishop Rosati. They discussed the needs of the German Catholics in the city. Bishop Rosati hoped that Father Helias could give some attention to this work. Not long afterward, the newcomer began to hold services for the Northside Germans in St. Aloysius Chapel of Saint Louis University. A few years later, Father John P. Fischer arrived to help Father Lutz. Again the Southside Germans attended Mass at the Cathedral.

In the meantime, Bishop Rosati had received a gift from the Leopoldine Foundation in Europe. Back in 1827, Bishop Edward D. Fenwick, a Dominican, had sent his vicar-general, John Frederick Resé, a native of Hanover, to recruit German priests and solicit funds for the church in Cincinnati. Resé, later bishop of Detroit, succeeded in meeting the Emperor Francis I of Austria, who encouraged the development of a society to help the Church in America. The emperor's brother, the Grand Duke Rudolph, Cardinal Archbishop of Olmutz, assumed the protectorate of this new society, called the Leopoldine Foundation. Over the next eighty years it collected close to a half-million dollars for the Church in America. The St. Louis Diocese was one of its chief beneficiaries. Father Resé also succeeded in fostering the growth of a similar mission-help society in the Kingdom of Bavaria.

Bishop Rosati wrote to the Leopoldine Society in 1837. He reported that the number of Catholics in the diocese—German, Irish, French, and American—had grown steadily. Two German priests assisted him at the Cathedral, and eighteen other priests who spoke German worked elsewhere in the diocese. Less than a year later, he reported continued progress and brought to the attention of the Leopoldine Foundation the advantages the Midwest offered to immigrants.

In the mid-1830s, German Catholics from Westphalia and Hanover settled in Clinton County, Illinois, about forty miles east of St. Louis. The settlers on this rich prairie land shortly numbered about fifty people and, in 1837, sent representatives to Bishop Rosati. He sent Father Henry Fortman to work among them a year later.

Bishop Rosati encouraged immigration to Missouri through his letters and correspondence with the Leopoldine Association in Vienna. The region of St. Louis had much to offer Catholic immigrants from Europe—freedom, opportunity, rich land, the basic organization of Catholic life, and no militarism. Besides these positive factors, nativists in other parts of the United States drove some Catholics to the Missouri Diocese, or so Bishop Fenwick of Boston thought when he wrote to Bishop Rosati in 1837, "The persecuting spirit that prevails here is driving all our best Catholics to your Missouri."[1]

When the St. Louis prelate wrote the Leopoldine Foundation again in 1838 acknowledging another substantial gift, he estimated that the city now had 2,000 German Catholics. Three priests at the Cathedral spoke German. Jesuits at St. Louis and St. Charles understood the language. Parishes at Ste. Genevieve and Westphalia in Missouri and in Clinton County, Illinois, had German pastors. Further, Rosati had sent Father August Brickwedde to Quincy, Illinois, as resident pastor.

By that time, German immigrants no longer flowed in gently, like the River des Peres in July, but surged like the Missouri River at flood tide. St. Louis had three German-speaking priests at the Cathedral—Fathers Joseph Lutz, John P. Fischer, and Gaspar H. Ostlangenberg. Jesuit Father Helias offered Mass for Northside Germans at St. Aloysius Chapel of Saint Louis University. Father John Henry Meinkmann, who had accompanied immigrants from Westphalia, served the needs of heavily Catholic Washington, Missouri, forty miles west of St. Louis on the south bank of the Missouri River. The Vincentian Father Franz Xavier Dahmen preached fluently to both the colonial French and the new-coming Germans in Ste. Genevieve, Missouri's oldest settlement on the Mississippi, fifty miles south of St. Louis. Belgian Jesuits from Florissant visited German-Catholic communities in St. Charles County and, on occasion, baptized and solemnized marriages.

By contrast, no German priest worked in New England at the time. In 1839 Boston had a congregation of sixty or more German families but no parish.[2] Cincinnati had two German priests at Holy Trinity Parish,[3] Detroit had one German clergyman at the Cathedral,[4] New York City had one German priest at St. Nicholas German parish and one at Transfiguration.[5] Philadelphia had one priest of German background.[6] In Baltimore, one German priest assisted at the Cathedral and one served a German immigrant parish.[7]

The first school for German Catholics began in 1838 on Third Street between Plum and Hazel, just south of the central district. The Jesuits stationed at the university supervised a second school on North Sixth between Green and Morgan.[8] In all schools, parents insisted on the use of the German language, among other reasons, as a factor in unity.

Since the construction of the Cathedral, the only Catholic church in St. Louis in 1840, left the diocese heavily in debt, Bishop Rosati decided to go to Europe to collect money. Before he left for the East, he blessed the cornerstone of St. Francis Xavier Church in conjunction with Saint Louis University on April 12, 1840. The Jesuits opened the church for services on Easter Sunday 1843.

Rosati set out, first, for the meeting of the bishops in Baltimore. After talking to Bishop Francis Patrick Kenrick of Philadelphia about releasing his brother, Peter Richard Kenrick, to be coadjutor bishop of St. Louis, Rosati boarded a boat for Europe. Pope Gregory XVI welcomed his countryman from St. Louis, approved his choice of co-adjutor (Father Kenrick, who reached St. Louis in 1841), and sent Bishop Rosati on a special mission to Haiti. Bishop Rosati served well in Haiti but died in Italy in 1843 on his return from the island.

In retrospect, the first bishop of St. Louis was as sure as the current of the Mississippi. What he set out to do, he did. He kept a diary, to the joy of historians. He wrote letters about the diocese to the Leopoldine Foundation that showed a commander-in-chief's grasp of far-flung campaigns. He had all the necessary characteristics of a missionary bishop: organization, zeal, discipline, dedication, and a way of dealing with his coworkers of all ancestries in a loving association.

Above: Bishop Joseph Rosati, C.M., first bishop of St. Louis.

✟ Chapter Three
Archbishop Kenrick Welcomes More German Catholics

Rosati's choice of successor, Peter Richard Kenrick, who became bishop in 1843, was a scholar rather than a pastor. One might have expected him to be bishop of Galway or Cork rather than of a small diocese on the American frontier. But during his years, St. Louis became more important than Galway or Cork, and an archdiocese before Boston, New York, or Philadelphia. Kenrick read widely and excelled as a theologian. He preached well and, in his early years in St. Louis, he traveled about Missouri. He stayed out of politics, refrained from telling Governor Hamilton Gamble how to run the state, and ignored Secretary of State Seward's concern about waving the flag over the Cathedral. He separated church and state absolutely.

As mentioned on a previous page, the Jesuits opened St. Francis Xavier Church, whose cornerstone Bishop Rosati had blessed before he left for Europe, on Easter Sunday 1843. The Irish on the near Northside invited Bishop Kenrick on October 17, 1843, to the northwest corner of Sixth and Biddle Streets, where St. Patrick's Church was to rise shortly. Ann Mullanphy Biddle gave the property. Her father John Mullanphy had left a thousand dollars for the building fund.

In a letter to Bishop Francis Patrick Kenrick of Philadelphia, the brother of the St. Louis bishop, the Central Council for the Propagation of the Faith reported that complaints had come in from Bavaria that bishops in various parts of the United States neglected the immigrants. No one could justly say that about Bishop Rosati. Nonetheless, Kenrick looked into the matter immediately.

On November 9, 1843, Kenrick reported to Archbishop Vincent E. Milde, the president of the Leopoldine Society in Vienna, that two Germans were stationed at the Cathedral. One worked exclusively with his fellow immigrants. He offered Mass and preached in German every Sunday and holy day. Some Germans worshipped at St. Aloysius Chapel in the Jesuit community at Saint Louis University and others at the Seminary of the Holy Trinity, staffed by Vincentians on the Southside. He estimated the number of German Catholics in the diocese to be 6,000, tripling the number in a few years.

Kenrick pointed out that the recently deceased Bishop Rosati had long planned to erect a large church for the exclusive use of German newcomers. The general population of St. Louis had increased with extraordinary rapidity. Soon no other nationality would match the Germans in number of immigrants. Kenrick told of the erection of the Jesuit church, St. Francis Xavier, where the German residents on the near Northside could attend Mass.[1] On March 17, 1844, Bishop Kenrick laid the cornerstone of St. Vincent's, on South Tenth and Park Streets. One of the architects was Meriwether Lewis Clark, son of the great explorer and general William Clark. Vincentians staffed this parish. Father James McGill was pastor of the English-speaking portion of the congregation, and the Reverend J. G. Euland pastor of the Germans. Father Euland held this post for many years, and three others—Fathers Herman Koop, Pius G. Krentz, and Henry Augustine Asmuth—served for shorter periods. Within a few years, the congregation numbered 6,000 persons.

People living midway between St. Vincent de Paul and the Cathedral needed a church. Ann Lucas Hunt, daughter of Judge J. B. Lucas, donated half a block at Third and Gratiot. Since it was a suitable site for a church, the diocese purchased the remainder of the block from her brother James Lucas for $2,500. Father John

Left: Peter Richard Kenrick.
Right: Joseph Melcher.

P. Fischer shepherded the flock of St. Mary's of the Victories. Bishop Antoine Blanc of New Orleans blessed the cornerstone on June 25, 1843, and the first Mass took place the following year on September 15, 1844. The second pastor was the vicar-general, Father Joseph Melcher, later Bishop of Green Bay. The third, the Reverend Henry Muehlsiepen, became the next vicar-general, and the fourth pastor was Father William Faerber, who was appointed in August 1868. By that time an addition had doubled the size of St. Mary's of the Victories Church.

Help kept coming for the expanding diocese. St. Louis received $17,600 directly or indirectly from the Leopoldine Society. Bishop Kenrick thanked the Austrians for their generous gift and wrote again on August 29, 1844, in appreciation of another gift toward St. Mary's Church of $1,450.[2] When one thinks that a church at that time would cost $6,000, the significance of these gifts comes into focus.

Northside Germans, who had been attending Mass in the St. Aloysius Chapel of Saint Louis University, joined their Irish neighbors for the laying of the cornerstone of St. Joseph's Church on April 14, 1844. Ann Mullanphy Biddle donated the lot to the German congregation. Two years later, the church of Ionic architecture, facing Eleventh at the northwest corner of Biddle, welcomed its congregation.

By late 1844, the German Catholics in St. Louis had three commodious churches: St. Joseph on the near Northside, St. Mary's of the Victories in the center, and St. Vincent de Paul on the southern part.

On December 10, 1844, Kenrick wrote again to Archbishop Milde, describing the state of Missouri and estimating the Catholic population at 50,000 souls, of whom at least one-third were immigrants from various areas of Germany. This population, he stated, was unequally dispersed over the state. The largest proportion was found near the Mississippi and Missouri Rivers. St. Louis was the chief city of the state of Missouri, increasing its population more rapidly than any other city in America. The state population was then between 35,000 and 40,000 souls, of whom at least two-fifths, if not one-half, professed Catholic religion. The entire German-Catholic population of the city could be set at 7,000 souls.[3]

Kenrick wrote with significance on December 10, 1844: "As no city in the United States enjoys greater opportunity for the practice of the Catholic religion, so there is none that expresses Catholic life and Catholic character better than St. Louis."[4]

As a result of the building of the Cathedral, the Panic of 1837, and the continued hard times that followed, the diocesan debt had been heavy. Then the building of five other churches further taxed the capacity of the Catholic people. In a decisive move, Bishop Kenrick relieved some of the financial burden by leasing for a hundred years the unused section of the church block not needed for church, rectory, or school.

The Cathedral had been the parish church for the entire city of St. Louis. On May 25, 1845, the bishop sent a pastoral letter to all Catholics, dividing the city into four ecclesiastical districts or parishes: the Cathedral, St. Francis Xavier, St. Patrick, and St. Vincent de Paul, and he set their boundaries. To meet the wants of the German portion of the Catholic population, included that within the Cathedral parish, he declared the church of St. Mary's of the Victories as a succursal church, or subsidiary chapel, to the Cathedral, for the German-speaking portion of its Catholic inhabitants and for these alone. When finished, the new church of St. Joseph would be a chapel of ease to the Germans living in St. Patrick's and St. Francis Xavier parish but only for the German people.

In this development, the archbishop made it clear that other nationalities, such as the Bohemian, Italian, Croatian, and Polish, would have similar succursal chapels for their people, even though they had no territorial limits. At first, it took care of the needs of these people. Later on, a better arrangement was needed so that the German

Right: St. Joseph German Church on Biddle at Eleventh, now a shrine.

and other pastors of national churches had the same rights as English-speaking pastors. Unfortunately, this did not occur under Archbishop Kenrick's rule.

When German Catholics moved into the North County in considerable numbers in the 1840s and 1850s, they could attend Mass and receive the sacraments at St. Ferdinand's Church in Florissant. At that time, to assist the Belgian pastor, Father Judocus Van Assche, and to provide spiritual assistance in their native tongue, the Jesuit Superior sent German-speaking priests, first Father Francis X. Horstmann and later Father Ignatius Panken.

In the early 1840s, seven families who lived along Mattese Creek in South County organized the Parish of the Assumption and built a log church. Among these seven families were two Fuchs brothers, Frederick and Johannes, who had reached St. Louis from the Rhineland via New Orleans in 1832, at the time the Cathedral was getting underway. In the old country they had grown grapes and learned the stone mason's craft. They worked on the new building, probably under John Withnell, who had the contract for the stone work. Offered land in the city or cash for their work, they chose the cash and bought a farm in Mattese. They farmed and began a vineyard. The Fuchs family grew, and over generations many remained in the area, as a visit to the parish graveyard will indicate.

Father John P. Fischer said Mass at the Church of the Assumption occasionally during 1842. Father Joseph Melcher served the area from 1844 to 1846. A native of Vienna, Austria, he had moved with his parents in his youth to Modena, Italy. He studied for the priesthood in Italy and was ordained in 1830. Bishop Rosati recruited him in 1843. It was one of the last acts of St. Louis's first bishop.

A brick church went up in 1848 at Mattese. Franciscan Sisters taught at the parochial school. The pastors had the further responsibility of looking to the spiritual needs of Catholics in Arnold, Missouri, on the other side of the Meramec River, among them the Telgmann, Poepper, and Klahs families from Westphalia. It proved to be a trying assignment. The parish challenged the zeal of seven pastors in the next ten years. Several transferred to other dioceses. One, Father Joseph Blaarer, pined for his Swiss mountains and went back to his native land. Another, Father Remigius Gebhard, a Bavarian, succumbed to cholera at age twenty-seven.

A number of German-Catholic families settled in Perry County, Missouri, from the 1820s through the 1850s: Schnurbusch, Baudendistel, Buchheit, Unterreiner, Wibbenmeyer, and others. Members of these families later moved to St. Louis.

During the 1840s, Jesuits at St. Joseph's, especially Father John N. Hofbauer, served as colonizers for those German immigrants arriving in St. Louis who wished to settle on farms. In contact by letter with their brethren in Franklin, St. Charles, and Osage Counties, the Jesuits directed new arrivals to those areas.

In 1846, Father Melcher visited Europe seeking priests and nuns for the diocese. At that time, he was named vicar-general for non-English-speaking parishes.

✝ Chapter Four
Early German Organizations Blossom

To help the poor, the Vincentian Superior John Timon challenged the laymen of St. Louis in 1846 to begin the first unit of the St. Vincent de Paul Society in America. It was the initial Catholic organization in St. Louis that went beyond parish and nationality. Of the eighty-nine men who took an active part in the society in its first six years, the president, Dr. Moses Linton, a convert, and nine others were Anglo-Americans, mostly from Kentucky and Maryland, spiritual director Father Ambrose Heim and ten others were German, five were French-American, and one was Slavic. The other officers and all of the other members were Irish or Irish-American.

Among the early German-speaking members were John Amend, Charles F. Blattau, Kaspar Brinkman, Joseph Broeken, John C. Degenhart, John Everhart, John Everhart, Jr., Dr. L. B. Ganahl, William Holterman, Philip Karst, Augustin Laufkotter, Christopher Pieper, Francis Saler, and H. J. Spaunhorst.

While still at St. Mary's of the Victories, Father Heim had encouraged his people to save. Many had found difficulties in borrowing money at low rates of interest. Further, many newcomers, not yet fluent in English, were suspicious of banks. They began to deposit their nickels and dimes in Father Heim's little bank. Gradually more and more parishioners put their money in Father Heim's care. Bishop Kenrick learned of these activities. He transferred the priest to the Cathedral in 1846 and made him his secretary. Father Heim anticipated the parish credit union by fifty years.

When people heard that the bishop of St. Louis was willing to accept any amounts on deposit and promised a fair rate of interest, money flowed in from all sides. The bishop set apart a small room in his residence for the banking enterprise. In the course of time he found it necessary to set up an office. At first, Father Heim handled details, but later the bishop hired a layman to assist. After the premature death of Father Heim, the archbishop with the assistance of laymen ran the bank successfully. The "Little Bank" of Father Heim became the "Large Bank" of Arch-

Left: Franz Saler, builder and backer of German-Catholic publications and active in many Catholic organizations.
Right: Valentine Reis I, President of St. Vincent's Orphan Society.

bishop Kenrick in 1850. In that year the balance rose from $588.69 on February 1, to $19,509.03 on December 31. The names of Francis Saler and other substantial businessmen appeared on the rolls.

A casual glance at the list of depositors in the early years shows the wide range of national origins: Bernard Schlangen, Joseph Strelciki, Arnold Van Hock, Lambert Vervoorst, Bernard Viktar, Bartolomeo Bernero, and Michael Brennan. Father Heim had done the Catholic community a distinctly needed and not-to-be-forgotten service.

In 1846 German Catholics started the German Catholic Benevolent Society to help the immigrants and others of the German language group. John Amend was elected president, Joseph Kulage vice president, Joseph N. Hendricks first secretary, and F. Wellmann treasurer. Their first public appearance in a body took place at the laying of the cornerstone of Sts. Peter and Paul. The founders incorporated the society in February 1849.

In that very month, cholera hit the city, and before the end of the year, it had taken one out of every ten persons. On June 12, 1850, Vicar-General Joseph Melcher and a committee of priests and laymen called upon the German Catholics of the city to form a society for the care of the orphans. The appeal resulted in the organization of the German St. Vincent's Orphans Society, with Frank A. Stuever president, J. F. Mauntel vice president, Francis Saler treasurer, Charles Blattau first secretary, and Edward Buss second secretary. On the death of President Stuever a month later,

Above: Girls' sewing class at St. Vincent's Orphans Home.

Valentine Reis succeeded him.

The Orphan Society took off like a steamboat moving with the current, and it soon had eighty-two members. In its name, Father John Elet, the Jesuit Superior, bought a lot on Hogan Street between Cass and O'Fallon, an area of the city that soon gained the name Kerry Patch. The German St. Vincent's Orphans Home, dedicated in May 1850, cost $5,980.00. The six incorporators were F. J. Heitkamp, B. Heidaker, J. Degenhardt, F. Heitkamp, J. F. Mauntel, and F. Beehler. Father Joseph Patschowski and three other Jesuits served as chaplains over the years. Five Sisters of St. Joseph took charge of the girls and boys.

Archbishop Kenrick authorized two collections annually at all the German churches in the city. St. Joseph's led the way on the first collection. As more German parishes grew in the city, all had a branch of the German St. Vincent's Orphans Society. Many congregations in outstate Missouri also contributed.

The Reverend Otto Hoog, the first graduate of St. Vincent's Orphans Home to become a priest, offered his first Mass at the orphanage in 1867. Eventually, he became vicar-general of the archdiocese.

Dr. Nicholas Guhman, a Bavarian-born graduate of Saint Louis Medical College, was in charge of St. Vincent's Orphan Home for eighteen years. He was assistant surgeon at the Vicksburg Hospital from the Confederate surrender there in 1863 to the end of the Civil War in 1865. A member of the Catholic Knights of America[1], he also served for four years (1869–1873) on the city school board.

✝ Chapter Five
The Coming of Germans of Other Faiths

erman Catholics were solidly established religiously in St. Louis before their Protestant countrymen began to organize. As late as 1837, German Protestants were yet to establish a church in St. Louis.[1] In 1833 Evangelicals had formed their first church in eastern Missouri in the area of Femme Osage in St. Charles County. During the following year, Evangelical Reformed in the city had established the congregation of the Holy Ghost that met at Benton School on Sixth Street between Locust and St. Charles. The Evangelicals opened a school in 1837.

While many Americans tend to think of German Protestants as Lutherans, as far as America was concerned a far greater number of Protestant Germans were Calvinistic Evangelicals, even the misnamed Pennsylvania Dutch. Almost all Germans in the colonial period were members of the Evangelical Reformed Church.

Lutheran immigrants from Saxony began to worship in the basement of Christ Episcopal Church in 1839. A short time later, they built Trinity Church in the eighteenth block of South Eighth Street and opened a parochial school in the area. The congregation grew strong under the leadership of the Reverend C. W. F. Walther. But more of the early Saxons lived around Altenburg in the southeast section of Perry County, where they opened Concordia Seminary. The seminary was to move to St. Louis in the 1850s. Eventually, the Lutherans conducted twenty-two schools in the St. Louis region.

In 1845 the Evangelical Reformed set up two congregations, the Northside church, St. Peter's, at Fifteenth and Carr, and a Southside church, St. Marcus, at Jackson and Soulard, just north of Lafayette Avenue. Eventually the Evangelicals opened the German Protestant Orphan Home, the Good Samaritan Hospital, and a seminary near Femme Osage in St. Charles County that later moved to St. Louis, and they developed twenty-eight congregations. They did not ordinarily maintain parish schools.

Events in Europe during the year 1848 affected the course of St. Louis history and of the German story in St. Louis in a profound way. Groups of Germans had hoped to unify their country by political action in 1848. In that year revolutions broke out all over Europe, in Paris, Brussels, Berlin, Prague, Naples, and Vienna. The efforts of these people to unite German states failed, chiefly because of the opposition of Emperor Franz Joseph of Austria, who had the backing of Czar Nicholas I of Russia. Many disgruntled Germans emigrated. A large percentage came to St. Louis.

These "Forty-Eighters," as they came to be called, allegedly to distinguish them from the "Dreissigers" (the "Thirtiers"), a term soon to drop from use, were better educated than the vast majority of immigrants. Some were professional men: teachers, lawyers, doctors, editors. One of them, Carl Schurz, eventually became U.S. Senator from Missouri. Having failed to unite Germany, the Forty-Eighters strongly supported the Union and would serve in great numbers when the South seceded. Missouri never needed a federal draft, so numerous were Union volunteers. The newcomers had been anticlerical and anti-Catholic in the old country, often identifying the Catholic Church with Austrian rulers. Some were anti-Jesuit in St. Louis, such as Heinrich Bornstein, the editor of the newspaper *Anzeiger des Westerns (Informer of the West)*.

Perhaps he used the term "Jesuit" for all Catholics, as many writers did at the time. Be that as it may, Bornstein also opposed conservative Lutherans, Sunday closing laws, and tax exemption for churches. Like Elijah Lovejoy before him, Bornstein could have gone to Saint Louis University and talked to the Belgian Jesuits, who had come to America for freedom from Dutch tyranny thirty years before, just as the Forty-Eighters had fled Prussian tyranny. Instead, Bornstein, like Lovejoy, criticized without taking time to get available information. A political result of such attacks by Bornstein's group was this: since their maligners joined the newly forming Republican Party, "many Germans in St. Louis, including conservative Lutherans and the majority of Catholics . . . remained with the Democratic Party."[2]

The nativists of the time, called by their own choice the "Know-Nothings," worked against immigrants elsewhere accepted the Forty-Eighters. In doing this they showed that anti-foreignism proved less a factor in St. Louis than their anti-Catholicism.

At that time, the public schools were getting started in America and grew up as a Protestant institution. They were quite acceptable to English-speaking Protestants, but hostile to Catholic beliefs and practices and against any effort at equality of educational opportunities for the Catholics or Lutherans who wanted their own religious schools.

The four German groups, Catholics, Evangelicals, Lutherans, and anticlerical Forty-Eighters, lacked a common rallying point, sharing only a common language and culture. Lutherans looked upon the Pope as the Anti-Christ, and Catholic writers berated Martin Luther. Evangelicals lacked ties with Lutherans and Catholics and eventually united with the English-speaking Congregationalists. The Forty-Eighters centered their lives on gymnastic and singing societies. They themselves apparently did not attend church. In fact, many looked on the Turner-Hall as the social and community center as Catholics, Evangelicals, and Lutherans looked to the parish hall. Even though German Catholics might at times have complaints about Irish Church leadership, the German Catholics at St. Joseph's felt closer to the Irish Catholics at St. Patrick's than to the Lutherans at Holy Trinity in Soulard.

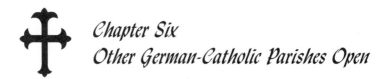

Chapter Six
Other German-Catholic Parishes Open

The Southside was expanding. By the census of 1850, there were 8,832 German-born residents in the First Ward, the area south of Chouteau Avenue that included the old French district called Soulard. The Germans constituted 64.6 percent of the ward's population. Even though Trinity Lutheran Church lay in that area, a large percentage were Catholics. Of these, 256 residents owned real estate averaging $1,436.26 in value.[1] They obviously intended to stay.

The area needed a Catholic Church. Father Simon Sigrist seemed to be the priest for the new parish. While pursuing clerical studies at Shrewsbury in Alsace three years before, Sigrist had responded to an invitation from Archbishop Kenrick presented by his recruiter, Vicar-General Joseph Melcher, to work in St. Louis. Archbishop Kenrick ordained Sigrist and sent him to work along the border of South County. He pastored flocks at Mattese and Arnold. After a year and a half, the archbishop sent him to begin the parish of Sts. Peter and Paul. Father Sigrist bought a lot on Eighth and Allen Streets and built a small frame church. Among the weddings he witnessed in 1848 was that of Johannes Klahs and Anna Catherine Poepper from his former parish in Maxville, Missouri.

Soon the congregation needed a more commodius building. The second church was of brick in the same place, with a seating capacity of seven hundred. The cornerstone was laid October 1, 1851, and the building dedicated in 1854. When Bohemian immigrants came to St. Louis in 1854, they worshipped at Sts. Peter and Paul until they could open their own church, St. John Nepomuk's. It was, incidentally, the first Bohemian church in the New World.

Father Sigrist was tall and impressive but unfortunately a poor financier. When the congregation went into debt, the archbishop assigned physically small but intellectually prominent Father Francis Goller as assistant. In his early years in the seminary, Goller had studied under some of the greatest teachers in Germany, and he was an extremely able theologian. A clash of views prompted the archbishop to move Father Sigrist and name Father Goller as pastor in 1858.

Father Sigrist transferred to the Diocese of Vincennes and took charge of a German parish in Indianapolis with greater success. Father Goller was to serve at Sts. Peter and Paul until his death. In 1870 the parish opened its own cemetery on Gravois Avenue that eventually became the resting place of most Southside Catholics.

On the city's Northside, the little community of Bremen, once, like Carondelet, independent but later absorbed by St. Louis City, needed a church. The closest church for the German Catholics of Bremen was St. Joseph's at Eleventh and Biddle, twenty-nine blocks to the south. In 1848 a committee explained its needs to Vicar-General Melcher. He thought the number of Catholics in the district far too small, but the committee went to see Archbishop Kenrick and explained conditions. The archbishop granted their request for a church at Eleventh and Mallinckrodt to be called Holy Trinity. While Forty-Eighters put the Catholics on the defensive, Protestant neighbors joined the building project with gifts of property. The parishioners built a one-story stone church.

In January 1849, the archbishop appointed Father Theodore Laurensen pastor. Father Laurensen didn't stay long, and neither did his successor, Father Joseph Blaarer. Father John Anselm, an exacting administrator, succeeded him in September 1850 and stayed five years. After Anselm's first year, baptisms rose from 71 to 155 and the number of marriages from 27 to 58. Assistants found it difficult to work with Father Anselm, and Father Caspar Doebbener became pastor. He organized a building society of ninety members for the purpose of gathering funds for a larger church. Archbishop Kenrick consecrated the second Holy Trinity Church in November 1859.

Many prominent families moved from the area of Clarholz in Westphalia, Germany, to Holy Trinity Parish. Among them were the Griesediecks, the Kreys, and the Muckermans. A more detailed look at one of the many Muckerman branches is in order here, as typical of the other Holy Trinity standouts.

Chris Muckerman, born in 1840, was the son of a German farmer who saw little opportunity in the homeland and urged his son to move to St. Louis, where his brothers John and Edward had preceded him. This he did in 1855, crossing the ocean to New Orleans and traveling up the Mississippi River. After the outbreak of the Civil War, he served mostly at one of the forts defending the city from Confederate raiders. The raiders never came, but the soldiers stood ready. After the war, Chris joined his two brothers in the Muckerman Brothers Ice Company.

When Edward left the firm to take up farming in Creve Coeur, John's and Chris's families lived in a duplex residence on North Fourteenth Street. Later, Chris bought out his brother John, then borrowed $350 from a merchant on Broadway to purchase an ice-wagon and a team of horses. He never looked back.

After a few years, he expanded by purchasing other ice firms. At length, two companies, headed by Charles L. Whitelaw, joined Muckerman to form the Polar Bear Ice and Fuel Company. Eventually, Whitelaw sold his interest and Chris Muckerman gained full control.

The area between Holy Trinity and St. Joseph's now needed a church. It was to bear the name of St. Liborius, a name not well known among the Carls, Ottos, Augusts, Henrys, and Hermans in St. Louis. But it was a familiar name among the residents of the area. St. Liborius, bishop of Lemans in the fourth century, was patron of the Diocese of Paderborn in Westphalia, the ancestral home of the people in the neighborhood. Many more were to come in the 1870s. They settled in the eighteenth block of North Eighteenth Street, between St. Joseph's at Eleventh and Biddle and Holy Trinity, twenty-eight blocks farther north. Under the leadership of a recent arrival from overseas, Liborius Muesenfechter, a group of Paderborners, asked Archbishop Kenrick permission to build a church and to assign a pastor for them. The archbishop said yes to both requests. He sent forty-year-old Father Stephen Schweihoff, himself a native of Paderborn, as pastor of the church on Hogan at North Market. He offered the first Mass in a small church in January 1857.

Above: John Thornton, benefactor of Catholic parishes of all nationalities.

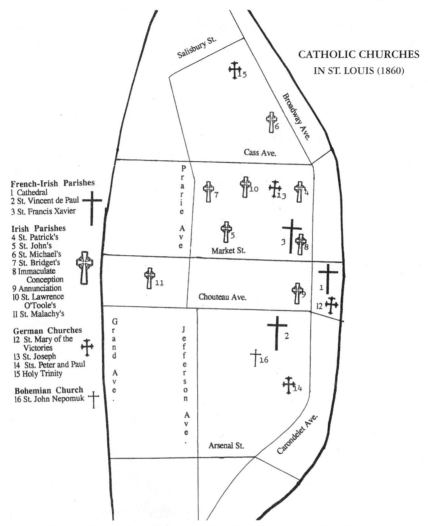

CATHOLIC CHURCHES
IN ST. LOUIS (1860)

Salisbury St.

Broadway Ave.

Cass Ave.

French-Irish Parishes
1 Cathedral
2 St. Vincent de Paul
3 St. Francis Xavier

Prarie Ave

Irish Parishes
4 St. Patrick's
5 St. John's
6 St. Michael's
7 St. Bridget's
8 Immaculate
   Conception
9 Annunciation
10 St. Lawrence
   O'Toole's
11 St. Malachy's

Market St.

Chouteau Ave.

German Churches
12 St. Mary of the
   Victories
13 St. Joseph
14 Sts. Peter and Paul
15 Holy Trinity

Grand Ave.

Jefferson Ave.

Bohemian Church
16 St. John Nepomuk

Carondelet Ave.

Arsenal St.

Above: The churches listed on this map benefited from the bequest of John Thornton.

A second generation would build a more impressive church in 1888 after many more Paderborners fled Bismarck's persecution and settled near them. Even later, St. Louis architect Joseph Conradi added an eighty-foot spire, modeled after that of the Freiburg Cathedral in their homeland. Early pastors came from Paderborn. Eventually, Father George Reis, a St. Louis native, gave great leadership to the parish.

The last pre–Civil War German parish in the city, named for St. Boniface in honor of the Apostle of Germany, faced west in the seventy-sixth block of South Michigan Avenue in Carondelet. Like all pre–Civil War churches, it lay a few blocks west of the Mississippi River. Vicar-General Melcher blessed the cornerstone in May

1860. Archbishop Kenrick dedicated the new church in December 1860. The parish was so poor that the contractor closed the church for debts. Father John Gamber had to ask Archbishop Kenrick for help to pay the bills.

These German parishes, as well as those of other immigrant groups, found unexpected help in 1858. A hitherto little-known St. Louis businessman, John Thornton, died and left almost a half-million dollars to the archdiocese. An immigrant from County Louth, north of Dublin, Ireland, he had prospered in merchandising and invested wisely in real estate in the neighborhood of Dubuque, Iowa. He had never married, left $10,000 to each of five nephews and nieces, and gave the rest to the Archdiocese of St. Louis. Archbishop Kenrick split the legacy in two, half in outright grants to Catholic schools, hospitals, orphanages, and old folks' homes, the other half a revolving fund for building churches. Each parish could secure an interest-free loan for an indefinite term.

St. Mary's, Sts. Peter and Paul, St. Boniface, and Holy Trinity shared in an early distribution of the Thornton Bequest: St. Liborius, St. Nicholas, and Holy Cross in later actions. While most of the parishes paid back only half of their shares of the Thornton Bequest, St. Mary's, Sts. Peter and Paul, and St. Nicholas paid back their borrowings with interest by 1862.[2]

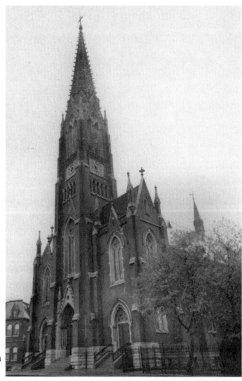

Right: St. Liborius, home of immigrants from Paderborn.

Chapter Seven
German Nuns in Education

When Vicar-General Joseph Melcher went to Europe in 1846 to recruit personnel for the Church in St. Louis, he met an Ursuline nun, Mother Magdalen Stehlin, at a convent near Vienna. She wanted to begin an institution of her order in the "wilds of America." Back then, when St. Louis stood near "Indian country," it must have seemed wild enough to her.

Saint Angela Merici had founded the order in Italy in the sixteenth century to instruct little children. It had grown amazingly in the following century, especially in France, and won great success. On his return to America, Father Melcher told Archbishop Kenrick of the possibility of securing Ursuline nuns from Europe. The archbishop heartily approved, and Father Melcher passed on his word of welcome. Two other nuns from the Austrian convent accompanied Mother Magdalen. On the way, they visited an Ursuline community at Landshut in Bavaria, gaining one novice and the promise of help from the sisters.

Archbishop Kenrick welcomed them at Baltimore and asked Father W. R. Wheeler to escort them to St. Louis. They arrived on September 5, 1848, and enjoyed the hospitality of the Visitation Sisters for two months. Then, the Ursulines moved into a small residence and opened a school. Seven nuns from Landshut enlarged the community. They brought $960 in donations with them. The Bavarian Mission Society, the *Ludwig Mission Verein*, a union of all Bavarian mission help societies under the sponsorship of King Ludwig I of Bavaria, promised support. The king personally gave $4,000 to purchase land for a new convent. Over the next seventeen years, the Ursulines would receive sums averaging $600 a year from the *Ludwig Mission Verein*.

The archdiocese purchased a plot of ground at Twelfth and Russell. Architect Francis Saler planned and built the new convent, the first Ursuline Academy in America. The nuns soon paid all bills. They later opened an academy in Arcadia, Missouri, and moved their St. Louis Academy to suburban Glendale. They later also opened parochial schools outstate. Since they were a cloistered order, they needed a special dispensation to live away from the convent. Archbishop Kenrick was able to arrange this privilege.

At the urging of the Redemptorist Fathers, Bishop Michael O'Connor of Pittsburgh sought a community called the School Sisters of Notre Dame from the motherhouse of Munich, Bavaria. The saintly Bishop John Neumann, Superior of the Redemptorists, had helped the sisters secure a house near St. James Church in Baltimore in October 1847. In 1850 Mother Caroline Freiss, the youngest of the sisters, was named vicar-general for America and went west to establish a western province with the center at St. Mary's Church in Milwaukee. Mother Caroline built up the western province with zeal and enthusiasm and a gentle sway.

In 1858 Father Joseph Patschowski, pastor of St. Joseph's Church, brought the School Sisters of Notre Dame to St. Joseph's. Mother Caroline opened the school on May 10, 1858, on land donated by Ann Mullanphy Biddle. Over the years, among other areas of excellence, girls from the school did such superb needlework that displays held places in musea a century later.

In the following fall, Father Francis Goller of Sts. Peter and Paul obtained three Notre Dames as teachers for the three hundred pupils in the parish school. On the same day, Father Stephan Schweihoff of St. Liborius Church entrusted his school of seventy pupils to the care of the Sisters of Notre Dame. The School Sisters also opened a convent near St. Mary's of the Victories. Extensive growth soon followed. American-born novices began to join along with immigrants. Later in the century, St. Louis became the seat of the southern unit of the School Sisters of Notre Dame with the motherhouse called Santa Maria in Ripa, on the Mississippi River, south of the city. The congregation expanded and had a distinguished role in archdiocesan development.

In 1859 three Franciscan Sisters came from Oldenburg, Indiana, to Holy Trinity Parish in St. Louis. They opened a school for girls there in early 1860.

In the meantime, Vicar-General Melcher, named bishop of Quincy, Illinois, and administrator of Chicago by Pope Pius IX, in 1853, sent the bulls back. He continued as vicar-general and visited Europe again in 1855. He succeeded in recruiting one priest, four sub-deacons and two theology students, among them Henry Muehlsiepen. He recruited again in 1866.

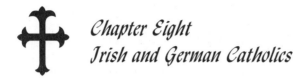

Chapter Eight
Irish and German Catholics

The presence of Irish and German Catholics in relatively equal numbers gave the Catholic Church in St. Louis a breadth of development unknown in most American cities. The two groups complemented rather than opposed each other. The Irish gave enthusiasm, the Germans stood for stability. The Irish opened new directions, the Germans "got the job done."

Germans came from the Northwest Provinces with either rural or urban skills. The urbanites worked at shops and breweries or opened their own. The "country boys" tilled "truck farms" in the suburbs and brought their produce to the Soulard or the North Market in the city. A number settled around Augusta on the north bank of the Missouri River, about forty miles west of St. Louis, and developed the wine industry. Eventually, Missouri became the third largest wine-producing state in the Union. Other newcomers came for "inexpensive fertile acres" and found unmatchable farmland in Clinton County, Illinois, just east of Belleville. As the century went on, the incredibly rich Florissant Valley beckoned them, and they formed a distinct parish, Sacred Heart.

Those Irish who came in the early American days (1804–1824) had experience in merchandising, the only business activity allowed the Irish under English law. They soon prospered in St. Louis, the merchandise center of the midcontinent. A few immigrants, among them John Mullanphy and Edward Walsh, gained relatively great wealth and became part of the "establishment" at the time of its forming, along with members of the French colonial families, such as the Chouteaus and the Soulards, and Anglo-Americans, among them the Clarks and the McKnights, who came from states along the Atlantic Coast.

During the late 1840s, a potato blight and English policy drove a million Irish to death of starvation at home and many more to new homes in America. The decade of 1850 to 1860 proved to be the high tide of Irish immigration to St. Louis. The

Germans kept coming and reached their peak several decades later.

These later Irish, fleeing the famine, had come chiefly from the less-fertile west-ern counties, such as Mayo. They had been tenants at the whim of the landowners and thus had no experience in the business of farming. Possessing no urban experi-ence, the Irish immigrant worked as a day laborer while he learned construction skills, carpentry, painting, or plumbing. Over the years, a few became contractors.

Both Irish and Germans favored the Democratic Party, at least until the Civil War, because the Republicans welcomed the anti-immigrant "Know Nothings."

While the leading Irish pastors tended to be public figures in the city, the out-standing German pastors were scholars, publishers of spiritual guidance, and influ-ential even among priests of other dioceses. The Irish pastor, coming from a country whose great cathedrals were "temporarily in the hands of the Anglicans," wanted to build a church. The German pastors, coming from a place where the parish church had gone up in the days of the Catholic Reformation (1530–1648), or before looked first to building and staffing a parochial school.

Several groups of German immigrants organized their own community, selected a site for the church, and asked for approval and a pastor. The Irish pastor received a pastoral assignment, then recruited parishioners. Laymen had more say in German parish organizations, while the Irish pastor usually made all decisions.

The German parish usually had a sign in front of the church, giving times of Masses. English law prohibited any public identification of the place where priests offered the Sunday Mass. As a result, many Irish parishes continued the "no-sign" practice in America.

How did the two Catholic peoples look on one another in the American situa-tion? Each looked on the other as not fully expressing authentic Catholicity. Further, it was easy for the newcoming Irish to consider themselves American, because, on arrival, they could speak the language, whereas they might look upon the longer residing American citizens, who continued to speak German, as foreigners.

Kenrick himself, who had become the first archbishop of the Midwest in 1847, occasionally shared this attitude. Even though the Belgian Jesuit Peter Verhaegen, president of Saint Louis University and administrator of the diocese in 1840, had been in America many years before him, Kenrick, at least on one occasion, referred to the Jesuit Superior as a foreigner. On the other hand, when recently arrived Irish complained that their assistant pastor at St. Patrick's, Father Charles Ziegler, was a "foreigner," Kenrick sent them packing back to Biddle Street. Father Ziegler, a native of Ste. Genevieve, was at one time the only American-born priest in the entire arch-diocese. A relative said that he spoke English "with a Kentucky twang."

In the wider picture, Kenrick's policy of gradual Americanization won him the title of "Father of the Immigrant." He allowed all immigrants the use of their own language but did not give territorial status to these congregations. He appointed vicar-generals for English- and for German-speaking people. Even though more priests of the archdiocese after mid-century were German than Irish, only one Ger-man-speaking priest of the archdiocese, Vicar-General Melcher, became a bishop, while six of Irish ancestry shepherded various dioceses and archdioceses, including Chicago and Philadelphia.

On the other hand, when Kenrick sought an auxiliary on the departure of Father Joseph Melcher to be bishop of Green Bay, Wisconsin, in 1868, he listed the secretary of the archdiocese, the above-mentioned Father Charles Ziegler, as his third choice, according to the procedure of the time. The other two recommendees were Vicar-General Patrick Ryan and the Vincentian rector of St. Mary's Seminary in Perryville, Missouri, the Very Reverend Edmund Hennessey, C.M.

In 1848 Kenrick wrote to his fellow bishop and close friend, Bishop John Purcell of Cincinnati, "I believe the exclusive promotion of Irish or American subjects will not have a favorable influence either on the discipline of the Church, or the reputation for impartiality."[1] He pointed out the heavily German-Catholic settlements in Southern Illinois. Nonetheless, he did not act on this view often enough in choosing diocesan clergy for bishoprics.

Among reasons for this was that few parish priests spoke both fluent German and English. A bishop in Belleville, Illinois, years later ran into unnecessary trouble with a predominantly Irish parish, St. Patrick's in East St. Louis, because he spoke no English.

Kenrick regularly sought qualified German-speaking priests of religious orders for dioceses with a predominantly German-speaking membership, such as Quincy, Illinois. Among them were the Jesuit Fathers Joseph Patschowski, pastor of St. Joseph's, and Peter Spicher, the spiritual director at Saint Louis University. Both men handled several languages. But Jesuit superiors were not always ready to release their able men, because these men had taken a public vow against accepting bishoprics.

The refusal of successive Jesuit Superior Generals in this regard had surprised Archbishop Kenrick's predecessor, Bishop Joseph Rosati. He pointed out that St. Ignatius, the Jesuit founder, had insisted on this vow for established European dioceses. He was not thinking of the far-flung mission frontiers. Archbishop Kenrick shared Rosati's concern. The needs of the universal Church should have outweighed the "practices of the Jesuits."

Toward the close of the 1850s, Archbishop Kenrick invited the greatest Jesuit home-missionary, the Austrian theologian and author, Francis Xavier Weninger, to give a series of fifteen missions in St. Louis. Father Weninger tailored his missions to separate groups: married men, married women, young men, young women, and children. He wrote books on the saints and heaven. His *Catholicity, Protestantism, and Infidelity* went into French, Italian, and Hungarian editions and won praise from Pope Pius IX. Signs in the sky often accompanied the Jesuit's preaching, as did miracles of healing. A famous one took place at St. Joseph's Church in St. Louis, a story that will come up later. His missions proved a boon to the young German-Catholic community in St. Louis.

During that same decade, John Amend, president of the Roman Catholic Benevolent Society, often spoke of the need for a nationwide German-Catholic organization. This idea prevailed in Baltimore in 1855 under the name *Central Verein*. The fifth annual convention of the *Central Verein* was held in St. Louis in 1860, and John

Amend won the presidency. From the early 1870s, the headquarters of the *Central Verein* remained in St. Louis. After John Amend, Senator Henry Spaunhorst succeeded as leader of that vital organization and served for many years. In his book, *The Conservative Reformers*, historian Philip Gleason of Notre Dame University spoke of Spaunhorst's reputation as "the leading German Catholic layman of his generation."[3]

In conclusion, the French colonial pioneers, the Marylanders, and other Anglo-Americans who moved west, and the two large immigrant groups, Irish and German, gave St. Louis the image of a multinational city. As a result, the Bohemians, Italians, Poles, and others coming later to the city, found it easier to fit in than did those who settled in other Catholic communities in the usually Irish-oriented American dioceses of the Northeast.

Above: Senator Henry Spaunhorst, legislator, president of the Central Verein.

✝ *Chapter Nine*
German Catholics and the Civil War

R arely does one hear a German Catholic mention that an ancestor fought in
the Civil War. Like the Forty-Eighters, German Catholics supported the
Union and opposed slavery. But while the Forty-Eighters came to America
chiefly for political purposes, the Catholics fled Prussian militarism imposed on their
ancestral provinces. Even though thousands of Missourians joined the Confederate
Army, so many volunteered for the Union Army that the state met its quota without
drafting anyone. Further, a large percentage of the German Catholics arrived after the
conflict. Few immigrants came during the hostilities.

An extensive discussion of the Civil War is beyond the scope of this book. However, the immediate concerns of the Catholic Germans in St. Louis demands our attention. A month after the South fired on Fort Sumter, the Missouri state militia, under General Daniel Frost, a veteran of the Mexican War, had its annual encampment
at the west end of the city, near what is now the Frost Campus of Saint Louis University. The outlook of the militiamen was certainly more pro-South than pro-North.
General Frost, a native of New York, opposed extremists on both sides. Further, he
had married into the Mullanphy family in St. Louis. General William Harney, already
a frontier hero and head of the Department of the West, was an uncle of Mrs. Frost.

When President Lincoln called General Harney to Washington, a drastic New
Englander, Captain Nathaniel Lyon, took charge of the area. On the presump-
tion that the militia encampment was called to take the arsenal at St. Louis and its
military supplies, General Lyon moved the supplies safely to Illinois. He then enlisted
at least three thousand German immigrants, mostly Forty-Eighters, members of the
Turner Society, to surround the encampment. General Frost was forced to surrender.

General Lyon then made a serious error in judgment in marching the impris-
oned men down Olive Street through a crowd of people, most of them sympathetic
to the militia. A man in the crowd fired on Lyon's men. Captain F. C. Blandowsky

fell wounded. Lyon's men opened fire in response and killed many civilians. None of them were German Catholics, according to the records of St. Bridget's Parish, whose pastor attended the victims.

Archbishop Kenrick called for peace and tranquility. Instead, riots broke out. Many St. Louisans compared the troops of General Lyon with the Hessians the British had brought over from Germany in the Revolutionary War. Eventually martial law was declared, and the city continued under duress during the remainder of the war.

Most of the Germans who had surrounded Camp Jackson joined the Second, Third, or Fourth Regiments of the Missouri Union Infantry. The state militiamen, a large percentage of them Irish Catholics, including General Frost, went south after their parole and joined the First Missouri Confederates. A war spirit swept the country.

President Abraham Lincoln insisted that the purpose of the war was the preservation of the Union, a political not a moral issue. To save the Union, he'd free no slaves, free some of them and not others, or free them all, if needed, to preserve the Union. When General John C. Fremont, head of the Department of the West, freed the slaves in Missouri in late 1861, Lincoln cancelled his action. The President did not want to alienate Union supporters who owned slaves.

As mentioned earlier, Archbishop Kenrick took a consistent policy of noninterference in political affairs. Unlike Archbishop John Hughes of New York and Bishop Patrick Lynch of Charleston, South Carolina, the St. Louis prelate made no public statement on the justice of either side. In this he had good company. When Pope Pius IX wrote identical letters to Archbishop Hughes and Archbishop John Odin of New Orleans, he urged a cessation of hostilities but made no comment on the morality of the conflict.

Archbishop Kenrick authorized no priest to join the army, so there was no German-Catholic priest in any of the St. Louis units to be a focus for Catholics and their participation. Father John B. Bannon, chaplain of the state militia, pastor of St. John the Evangelist Church on Sixteenth at Chestnut, and a native of Ireland, gave up his pastorate in favor of his chaplain's duties. He realized that the archbishop could find another priest to serve that excellent parish, but there was no one to take care of the many Irish Catholics in the first Missouri Confederate Brigade. In fact, the only other priest in the entire Confederate Army of the Trans-Mississippi was a man of French ancestry, Pere Felix Dicharry of the Third Louisiana Infantry.

Among the Missourians, Colonel Frank Von Phul was the one Catholic of German ancestry whose name appears in the Diary of Father Bannon or in books about the priest-chaplain. The only Confederate chaplain of German ancestry was a Benedictine, Emmeran Bliemel of the Tenth Tennessee, an Irish unit. Major James Utz of Florissant was hanged as a Confederate spy on December 26, 1864, at the Gratiot Street Prison (the old McDowell Medical College) in St. Louis. A commutation of the death penalty came from President Lincoln a day late. Military records show that a Father Ward, a Catholic priest, attended Utz spiritually in prison and on the scaffold. No other record connects Utz with the Church. Further, the *Catholic Almanac* for 1864 lists no Father Ward anywhere in the country.[1] The Utz home still stands on

Utz Lane in North County.

Among Union officers from St. Louis, the best-known names, Generals Franz Sigel and Peter Osterhaus, appear in no currently available Catholic record. Shortly after the war, they left the city permanently. Among the few clearly identifiable German-Catholic combatants, riverboat captain Benjamin Tannrath, father of the future chancellor of the archdiocese, John Tannrath, was a captain in the Union reserve. Michael Treinen, son of an immigrant, was a scout in Sherman's Army, and Bernard Faulstich, a baker. Three Heim brothers served in the Home Guards, as did Franz Josef Harke, a blacksmith from Paderborn who had settled in St. Liborius Parish and was married there in 1862 to fellow immigrant Wilhelmina Perne. After the conflict, he tilled a farm in Pine Lawn.

After the war, one Southern chaplain, the Redemptorist Aegidius Smulders, a Hollander who had served with the Eighth Louisiana Confederate Infantry, received a call to St. Alphonsus (Rock) Church on North Grand. He was the only priest chaplain to serve in St. Louis after the war.

A few Confederates, who had resided in St. Louis before the War, soon returned, among them Generals Sterling Price and Daniel Frost. Veterans groups organized as the Grand Army of the Republic and the United Confederate Veterans. No German Catholics from St. Louis led either group.

The Civil War split many Protestant denominations into Northern and Southern branches. The Catholic Church remained united. In fact, the bishops of the country met in the Second Plenary Council at Baltimore just eighteen months after General Robert E. Lee's surrender. Prelates like Archbishop John Hughes of New York and Bishop Patrick Lynch of Charleston, both vocal in defense of their sections, met together to patch up the wounds. The bishops looked at the problems facing the four million Catholics honestly and frankly. Most of the council decrees tended to harmonize church procedures throughout the country.

✝ Chapter Ten
New Churches

In spite of the wartime restrictions in a city under martial law, new churches went up. St. Boniface in Carondelet, which had closed for lack of funds, righted itself under its second pastor, energetic Father Ernest A. Schindel. At the same time, jobs had opened in the neighborhood, especially at the shipyards of James Buchanan Eads. In that Carondelet locale, Eads built the gunboats that helped General Grant open the Mississippi to Union control. Some parishioners of St. Boniface worked there. Archbishop Kenrick advanced $15,000 of the Thornton Bequest to the parish. At first he had asked 6 percent interest, gradually lowered the rate, and finally, in 1870, he remitted all debt for all parishes that had paid at least half of what they owed. St. Boniface had paid only one-fifth. The archbishop remitted $11,630.81.[1]

When the parish needed a new school, Father Schindel sold 205 shares at $25 a share. Each year a public drawing paid back 20 shares. Before all 205 were paid, 44 shareholders had donated their shares. School Sisters of Notre Dame taught at St. Boniface School from 1866 to 1879, the Sisters of St. Joseph filled in for a year, and then the Sisters of Christian Charity carried on.

The names of many residents of St. Boniface remained in the news, especially the Lammerts, dealers in fine furniture, the Hoffmeisters and Fendlers, funeral directors, and the Winkelmanns, druggists.

About thirty-five blocks north of St. Boniface, in February 1863, the Franciscan Fathers planned a parish in conjunction with their new priory on Meramec, recently completed by John Withnell, a prominent St. Louis businessman and benefactor of Catholic institutions. The friars held services for prospective parishioners in the chapel, beginning August 2, 1863. Father Servatius Altmicks, O.F.M., organized the parish. Archbishop Kenrick laid the cornerstone of the church, facing north, on Meramec at Kansas Avenue, on April 10, 1864. Bishop John Hogan of St. Joseph, Missouri, blessed the new church five years later. Father Servatius also began the first

Left: Fr. Ernest A. Schindel, Pastor of St. Boniface Church (1861–1895).

unit of the Third Order of St. Francis in St. Louis. In this society, laymen pledged to follow the spirit of St. Francis in their daily lives. Some of the most distinguished men of various parishes and backgrounds joined the Third Order.

At the northern reaches of the city at that time, Archbishop Kenrick had a summer residence in a section of Calvary Cemetery. Catholics in the neighborhood, among them the Stapenhorsts, often attended Mass in the chapel there. Father Caspar Doebbener, Rector of Holy Trinity, asked permission to form a new parish from that distant section of his parish. He blessed the cornerstone in 1863 and a year later offered Mass at Holy Cross Church. Among early families, these were active: Kraft, Kulage, Kehlenbrink, Vogels, Albers, Strauss, Bittner, Eckert, and Wieck.

On the near Northside, St. Joseph's parish continued to grow. Over the years, many prominent Jesuits served there, among them Fathers Arnold Damen, Joseph Patschowski, Francis Xavier Wippern, and Martin Seisl. A spiritual writer and editor, Father Seisl set up his own printing press and put out a weekly paper, *Sontag's Blatt* (*Sunday's Leaf*), and later the *Herold des Glaubens* (*Herald of Faith*). Father Seisl later served at St. Francis Borgia Parish in Washington, Missouri, where the Knights of Columbus Council bears his name. Archbishop Kenrick recommended Father Patschowski for the bishopric of Quincy, Illinois.

In 1865 the archbishop blessed the cornerstone of a new structure for St. Joseph's people. The old building facing Eleventh Street became the entrance of the new church that faced Biddle. A year later, the famous missionary, Father Peter John De Smet, at the time Jesuit Mission Promoter, celebrated the Mass of Dedication. Eventually, a new building used the old church as an entrance. It faced Biddle and stretched back along Eleventh. In 1880 a new facade with twin towers was added,

Left: St. Boniface.

making the dimension of the whole edifice 112 x 180 feet. A church of massive proportions with a Romanesque exterior and a Baroque interior, it seated 2,600 people. The parish registered 21,000 confessions in a single year. It enjoyed a unique destiny.

The great preacher Father Francis Xavier Weninger returned for another weekly mission. At the end of each talk, he blessed the ill with a relic of Peter Claver, a Spanish Jesuit missionary to black slaves in colonial Latin America, whose cause of beatification had been advanced in Rome. Claver's story was well known in the parish. While on the staff at St. Joseph's a decade before, Father Martin Seisl had written a life of the missionary and often spoke of him.

Among the parishioners blessed with the relic by Father Weninger, Ignatius Strecker* lay close to death due to cancer from a bone injury at work. After the blessing, Strecker readily regained his strength. No aftereffects remained of his injury. His physician, a Lutheran, attested to the unusual circumstances of his cure. It was one of the two miracles presented to Rome to bulwark the claim to sancity of St. Peter Claver. St. Joseph's gained permanent acclaim as the "altar of answered prayers."

St. Nicholas Church, at Twentieth and Lucas Street, began with the cornerstone laying by Archbishop Kenrick on April 29, 1866. The church was dedicated a year later. Of early English Gothic style, it was helped by a loan of $16,000 from the Thornton Bequest.

---

*Archbishop Ignatius Strecker of Kansas City, Kansas, was a grandson and namesake of the beneficiary of the miracle.

Ten German Catholics who lived southwest of Sts. Peter and Paul met in 1867 to discuss the need for a new parish in their neighborhood. They gathered at the home of Theodore Thien, an immigrant from Ermsland in northwest Germany. The conferees agreed and referred their hopes to the archdiocesan offices. A brick church went up on Ohio Avenue near Gravois Road, and the first Mass was celebrated on Christmas Eve. According to family recollection, Thien's youngest daughter Catharine was the first baptism at St. Francis de Sales Parish.

In early 1866 representatives of thirty-five German families in Florissant Valley came together to discuss the possibility of a church and school of their own. A delegation conferred with the Jesuit Provincial, Father Ferdinand Coosemans, and Archbishop Kenrick on their hopes. Both responded favorably. A huge crowd that included Sodalities, benevolent societies, and bands gathered for the cornerstone laying of Sacred Heart Church on June 3 of that same year (1866). Archbishop Kenrick spoke in English and Father Joseph Weber, S.J., of St. Joseph's Church, in German.

Following the typical German way, the people built the school first. It opened on September 15 at the time the foundation of the church was laid. In late October, the pastor, Father Ignatius Peuckert, S.J., invited Father Peter John De Smet, the colorful missionary, to bless the church on October 5, 1867. The archbishop was visiting Europe at the time.[2]

At this juncture, in July 1868, Pope Pius IX named Vicar-General Melcher bishop of Green Bay. This time he accepted the challenge. His assistant at St. Mary's of the Victories, Father Henry Muehlsiepen, became vicar-general in his place. An 1855 recruit of the new bishop, the energetic and affable Muehlsiepen had finished his studies in St. Louis, and Archbishop Kenrick had ordained him in 1857.

In 1866 Father Muehlsiepen co-founded the publication *Pastoral-Blatt* (Pastoral Pages), a journal for priests. In 1868 he gave up his parochial duties to concentrate on his task as vicar-general and his expanding role as a leader among priests of German background throughout the nation. He resided at the Ursuline Convent at Twelfth and Russell. In his priorities, he emphasized school before church and urged his people to follow that norm. They did. Men of St. Mary's, under the leadership of Charles F. Blattau, a member of the St. Vincent de Paul Society, voted to aid the children of penniless parents in pursuit of religious instruction. The new vicar-general welcomed two congregations of religious women to St. Louis, the Sisters of Mary and Sisters of the Most Precious Blood.

One of the parishes Father Muehlsiepen helped to organize, Our Lady of Perpetual Help on Fourteenth and Linton, began in 1873 with forty families from the northern section of Holy Trinity Parish. Another Northside church, St. Augustine's, went up at the southeast corner of Twenty-Second and Hebert Street, northwest of St. Liborius.

By 1876 the centennial of the Declaration of Independence, the German Catholics of St. Louis, with help from the Thornton Bequest, had opened a dozen churches. Perhaps the most beautiful was Gothic Sts. Peter and Paul that went up, according to Father Goller's plans, on the old site on Seventh at the northeast corner of Allen.

Neighboring pastors chided Father Francis Goller for building such an elaborate and beautiful structure. He responded that his people saw nothing but plainness during the week; he wanted them to see beauty on Sunday. This seemed to reflect the opinion of so many others, if we may judge from the significant clergymen who attended the dedication ceremony on December 12, 1875.

Bishop Edward Fitzgerald of Little Rock spoke in English and Bishop Francis Xavier Krautbauer of Green Bay in German. Coadjutor Archbishop of St. Louis, Patrick J. Ryan, conducted the ceremony of consecration, and Coadjutor Archbishop Michael Heiss of Milwaukee offered the High Mass. Other noted clergy in attendance included Bishops Louis Fink of Leavenworth, Kansas, and Rupert Seidenbusch, O.S.B., of Duluth, Minnesota, and Fathers Christian Wapelhorst and William Faerber.

In his early years in the seminary, young Goller studied under some of the greatest teachers in Germany. He was an extremely able man intellectually and theologically. He brought in the School Sisters of Notre Dame, the second community of that excellent religious congregation in the archdiocese. The sisters obviously have had no regrets, because over the years 160 members of their congregation came from the schools of the parish that had an average attendance of 1,300 pupils. Later, in 1897, the Brothers of Mary arrived to teach boys at the school.

Father Goller, one of the theologians of Archbishop Kenrick at the Third Plenary Council of Baltimore, spoke strongly of parochial schools. The council itself urged such schools throughout the country. Monsignor John Rothensteiner, in his history of the archdiocese, assures us that Father Goller was not the only member of the council that fought for parochial schools, but he certainly was one of the most effective.

The pro-parochial school forces prevailed. By 1898 St. Louis boasted forty parishes with schools. One hundred and forty-eight teachers taught 6,534 pupils in 21 English-language schools. One hundred and fifty-nine teachers taught 8,118 pupils in German-language schools. Further, the interparochial academies for girls and Christian Brothers College and Saint Louis University for boys taught many others.[1]

While these new churches and schools were blossoming, another sisterhood came from Germany to teach. Sisters of the Precious Blood had come to Southern Illinois in 1870 at the invitation of Bishop Henry Juncker. A dispute arose with his successor, Bishop Peter J. Baltes. The superior, Sister Augusta, refused the bishop's condition that all the property must be held as diocesan property.

She got in touch with Vicar-General Henry Muehlsiepen in St. Louis, and twenty-one sisters moved across the Mississippi and accepted the school of St. Agatha Parish and two outstate schools. They planned a motherhouse at O'Fallon. By this time, Bismarck's *Kulturkampf*, his anti-Catholic, autocratic, and militaristic drive for German uniformity, had restricted the activities of the nuns. The entire congregation looked to the New World. Forty-nine sisters set out for the United States in August 1873, and they arrived in New York the following month. The Catholics of O'Fallon gladly welcomed them.

In the meantime, a group of sisters, the Adorers of the Precious Blood of Christ (A.S.C.), had remained in Illinois under the direction of Mother Clementia. They accepted Bishop Baltes' conditions and set up their own motherhouse at Ruma, the new name of the pioneer Irish settlement of O'Harasburg, about forty-five miles southeast of St. Louis. Thus, two distinct sisterhoods of Precious Bloods grew up within the radius of fifty miles of St. Louis.

The Sisters of the Most Precious Blood (C.PP.S.), of O'Fallon, Missouri, taught on the elementary and high school levels. The Ruma Sisters early opened a residence on the Saint Louis University campus. Several nuns from Ruma taught at the university, and one, Mother Catherine Girrens, A.S.C., became superior general of the entire sisterhood.

During the years when the Sisters of the Most Precious Blood were finding their way in the St. Louis region, many societies with uniforms, rituals, and secret oaths spread throughout the country. Church leaders questioned Catholic membership in these brotherhoods. Inspired by a sermon of his Bishop Patrick Feehan, James J. McLaughlin, a layman of Nashville, Tennessee, split with a secular society and set out to form the first Catholic fraternal society in the country. A man of average means and above-average zeal, McLaughlin convinced eight friends to join. First called the Order of United Catholics, at the bishop's suggestion, they took the name Catholic Knights of America. The multinational Knights offered insurance plans, organized spiritual and cultural activities, supported foreign missions, and encouraged religious vocations. In 1877 the organization won a charter from the state of Tennessee. The Knights spread to Kentucky, Ohio, Indiana, Missouri, and other states. The first branch in Missouri opened at St. Patrick's Parish in 1879. Other branches soon began chiefly in German parishes.

Above: Catholic Knights in their full regalia.

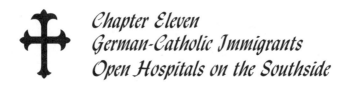

Chapter Eleven
German-Catholic Immigrants
Open Hospitals on the Southside

The Daughters of Charity, mostly of Irish background, had begun the first hospital in St. Louis and later started two others. The first hospital in the German-Catholic community was founded by the Alexians, a men's healthcare congregation, little known beyond the area of the German-Belgian frontier.

The people of St. Louis had known Jesuits, such as Father Sebastian Meurin, from French colonial days, the Vincentians from territorial days, through the arrival of Bishop Rosati and his fellow Vincentians, mostly from Italy, and, in the 1850s, the Christian Brothers from Ireland. They, too, belonged to a well-known congregation. Shortly after the Civil War, Alexian Brothers came to St. Louis. Who were these Alexians, members of a congregation utterly unknown to St. Louisans? They had existed since the Middle Ages, never numerous, but enduring. A "grass roots movement," they looked back to no inspiring leader such as Sts. Benedict, Francis, Dominic, Ignatius, or Alphonsus, who gathered followers around them to form religious orders and congregations. The congregation took root in various places out of the generosity of many men.

In the Middle Ages, in towns of Belgium and Germany, individuals visited the sick, buried the dead, called priests to the ill who needed them, and consoled the relatives of those who died. As time went on, they formed groups and lived near hospitals. During the terrible "Black Death" of 1349, even though most people wanted to flee, they stayed to help, to visit the sick, and to bury the dead. This brought them to the attention of town councils and later to princes and bishops. Eventually, after they had served their neighbors for a century, Pope Sixtus IV approved the brothers in 1472. All members stood on the same level in the early days. No priests were members. The brothers sought the guidance of priests from their parishes and from various religious orders.

Shortly after the Civil War, the Alexians sought to locate a hospital in St. Louis.

The pioneer Alexian Brother Bonaventure Thelen had served in hospitals in Germany and also on the battlefield in the short Danish-Prussian War of 1864. Brother Bonaventure felt a call in prayer to work in America and urged his superior to authorize him to answer that call. Even though his own determination pushed the superior into the decision, Brother Bonaventure insisted upon being ordered to go to America so he would have the full value of obedience.

Shortly before his ship reached New York, it sank. No one drowned, but most people lost their luggage. Brother Bonaventure lost his letter of greeting to bishops in America. When he finally received a renewed statement of his good intentions, he came to St. Louis and won the approval of Archbishop Peter Richard Kenrick. But before St. Louis Germans had a chance to consider what he planned to do, he made a circle of St. Louis, Milwaukee, and Cincinnati. At length, he started a small hospital in Chicago. Before that enterprise was well along, he planned to open a second hospital, this one in St. Louis. Archbishop Kenrick renewed his word of welcome. Brother Bonaventure started a small hospital in the old Simmons mansion on South Broadway. He purchased the residence from a successful businessman, James Lucas of French ancestry. Lucas gave a thousand dollars of seed money to open a drive that Brother Bonaventure undertook for funds.

The Simmons mansion provided the brothers with rooms for themselves and for ten to twelve patients. The building lay a block south of the city limits, but it was annexed by the city, along with the rest of Carondelet, within a year. It lay in the parish of St. Anthony of Padua, two blocks to the south and eight blocks west. During the hospital's early years, Franciscan Fathers Servatius Altmicks and Raynor Dickneite served as chaplains.

The brothers admitted their first patient on April 12, 1870. Within eight months, fifty-nine men had come under their care. They established a policy that the door of the hospital would be open day and night to anyone who needed their services. News of the excellent nursing skills of the brothers spread rapidly throughout the area. The little hospital had met a real need in the city of St. Louis. It served the Catholics in a heavily German immigrant area of the city. The Lutherans soon moved their seminary from Altenburg in Perry County to Jefferson Avenue, not far away from the Alexian hospital. They organized a congregation in the neighborhood, set up a publishing house, and eventually established their own hospital.

While the Alexian hospital in St. Louis continued steadily, the Franco-Prussian War of 1870–1871 left the European hospitals in turmoil. The Great Chicago Fire of 1871 destroyed the Alexians' hospital in Chicago.

In St. Louis, a new hospital went up on the site of the old on South Broadway in the 1870s. Vicar-General Muehlsiepen laid the cornerstone on Pentecost Monday, June 8, 1873. While considered a two-story structure, the new building in reality contained four levels, with a ground floor and an attic. In line with building practice common in Germany and in some St. Louis structures at the time, rooms ran down one side of the corridor only. A horse-drawn trolley on Broadway made access to the hospital simple for the people of the area.

In the early years, the hospital gained recognition because of its effort in eliminating the stigma associated with mental diseases. Previously, psychiatric hospitals were separate institutions. The Alexians included a psychiatric division within the general hospital. At the same time, the Alexians looked on the alcoholic as a person to be cured rather than one to be condemned. In short, the Alexian Brothers pioneered in the treatment of mental illness and alcoholism. The hospital's staff gave no sign of moral disapproval associated with alcohol. They looked upon it as a psychologically related disease. The psychiatric division gradually became a prominent sector of the hospital under the care of Dr. F. J. Lutz.

The Alexians celebrated Independence Day, July 4, 1874, by inviting Coadjutor Bishop Patrick Ryan to dedicate the new hospital. The choice of day was certainly patriotic but hardly wise if the brothers wanted to draw a large crowd. Most people had gone down to the riverfront to see General William Tecumseh Sherman, the Civil War hero, open James Buchanan Eads's beautiful bridge connecting St. Louis with Illinois.

In the meantime, Catherine Berger, a wealthy girl in Bavaria educated by the Ursulines, manifested a strong desire to enter the convent. Her mother opposed the move. Eventually, she won her mother's approval and entered a Franciscan community in her native land. In 1857 she received the habit and the name Odilia. With five other sisters, she went on a begging tour and then set up a convent in Paris. The sisters nursed the sick and kept a home for girls out of employment. All went well until the Franco-Prussian War forced them to move back to Germany, where they took care of wounded soldiers in a military hospital. They found that the hospital would soon close, and at that time, Chancellor Otto von Bismarck of the newly united German Empire began to limit the rights of Catholics and other groups.

Left: Mother Odilia Berger, Foundress of the Sisters of Mary, opened hospitals in St. Louis and outstate.

Mother Odilia and her little band of five sailed from Hamburg for America. They made arrangements to work in St. Louis and arrived on November 6, 1872. Vicar-General Muehlsiepen welcomed them and entrusted them to the guidance of Father William Faerber of St. Mary's of the Victories Church on South Third Street. The Ursuline Sisters offered them hospitality. Shortly, these Franciscan Sisters rented a tenement house opposite St. Mary's Church and offered needed health services. Smallpox had hit the city with great violence. In the meantime, three candidates arrived in St. Louis and joined the congregation. Others soon followed.

The increase in number of applicants forced the need for larger quarters. The sisters planned their own convent on a vacant lot south of St. Mary's Church in the spring of 1872. Mother Odilia went on begging tours that proved successful. In the fall of 1873 the building was completed, and Vicar-General Henry Muehlsiepen blessed the convent on the feast of St. Teresa, October 15. Fifteen sisters took possession of their first motherhouse in the New World. Since the people of the area called them "Sisters of Mary," they took that name and later added "of the Third Order of St. Francis."

In the next three years, more novices applied and required larger quarters. Mother Odilia looked to a ten-acre tract on Arsenal at Arkansas, just east of Tower Grove Park. A large brick building and two smaller buildings stood on the property, the gift of a generous lady, Mrs. Elizabeth Schiller.

When a yellow fever epidemic broke out in the South in 1878, the Sisters of Mary offered their services. Five left for Memphis in August, and a month later three others did. At the request of Bishop John Elder of Natchez, five sisters worked in Canton, Mississippi, where the plague was also raging. Of the thirteen sisters who went South, five died of the disease, and the remaining eight, although having contracted it, recovered and returned to St. Louis.

Naturally, the shock of losing five of their sisters was a blow to the community. Father Faerber, in Paris at the time, wrote a letter extolling the sisters for their great work in the South. In 1880 the Sisters of Mary received the approval of the new Pope, Leo XIII. On the feast of St. Francis of Assisi, October 4, Vicar-General Muehlsiepen accepted the vows of the sisters.

Over the years, the Sisters of Mary opened outstate hospitals at St. Charles and at Sedalia. They also conducted the Missouri Pacific Hospital from 1884 to 1889, and during the epidemic of smallpox the health commissioner of the city of St. Louis requested the sisters to nurse smallpox patients at the Quarantine Hospital. Two sisters fell to the disease. The sisters opened St. Mary's Infirmary on Papin Street, just south of the Union Station, on Lincoln's Birthday in 1889. The date of the blessing may have been prophetic. In a later chapter, the infirmary will take a step in line with Lincoln's initiative. This and other health ventures of the Sisters of Mary will come up in a later chapter. In the interim, Mother Seraphia Schloctmeyer planned a trip to Germany in 1892 to give possible candidates a look at the work of the sisters. As a result of this first visit, thirty young women embarked for St. Louis. Eventually, recruiting tours brought 138 candidates from Germany and other countries.

Another group of Franciscan Sisters came from the Province of Paderborn in northwestern Germany at the same time Mother Odilia's group came from Bavaria. In the 1870s, prodded by Chancellor Bismarck's anti-Catholic laws, more Paderborners came at the invitation of Father Ernest A. Schindel, pastor of St. Boniface Church in Carondelet, and found homes in St. Louis. Father Schindel hoped to provide a hospital for the sick poor of the parish.

Three Franciscan sisters arrived in 1872 and opened a hospital the following year. Two years later, a second company of eight nuns arrived. Some others, en route from Germany, went down on the ill-fated steamer *Deutschland* that sank in the estuary of the Thames River. Thomas Cardinal Manning gave an often-quoted sermon at a memorial service for the sisters in England. English poet Gerard Manley Hopkins wrote one of his more noteworthy poems, "The Wreck of the *Deutschland*," to commemorate the tragic event and the generosity of the sisters.

The Franciscan Sisters opened schools in outstate Missouri and a second hospital in Cape Girardeau. Gradually, the St. Louis foundation of the community became the center of a province. The sisters eventually set up a motherhouse adjoining the newly erected St. Anthony Hospital at Grand Boulevard and Chippewa Street in 1900.

Chapter Twelve
Some German Catholics in Business

St. Louis German Catholics entered a wide variety of businesses, and their leadership skills helped shape the future of many local industries. This chapter will list a random sampling of typical German-Catholic businessmen in St. Louis at the end of the nineteenth century, giving the place of their origin, some of their experiences, and items of interest about them. This is not inclusive, but rather typical.

Frederick Arendes was born in Westphalia in 1834 and came to St. Louis in 1849. He became the first president of Lafayette Bank in 1872 and continued until his death in 1898. He was well respected, a member of the St. Vincent de Paul Society and various other associations, and a sufficiently distinguished citizen of St. Louis that Mayor Henry Ziegenhein was an honorary pallbearer at his funeral.

James Baumgartner was a native of Maryland of Germanic background. He came to St. Louis in 1839, involved himself in general merchandising, and then moved into real estate and insurance. A Democrat and a Catholic, he was Deputy U.S. Marshal during the Civil War.

Michael Best, a Bavarian, was born in 1829 and came to St. Louis in 1852. He was involved in steamboating on Western rivers. He was one of the few Catholic Germans who served in the Civil War, in two outfits of the Union Army. After the war, he became a flour and feed merchant on South Broadway.

Theodore Beyert was born in Germany, province unknown, in 1833. He came to St. Louis and worked his way up from a retail grocery to a flour and feed store, which he opened at 4994 Natural Bridge. A Republican and Catholic, Beyert left a fortune, one of the many German businessmen who did so.

John Ganahl, of Tyrolese ancestry on both sides, was born in 1838 and came to St. Louis in 1856. He worked on the German-Catholic newspaper *Tages-Chronik*, sponsored by Francis Saler. He became a member of the city council and was highly successful in the lumber business and prominent in Catholic organizations.

Andrew Geisel, a merchant and manufacturer, was born in Hesse-Darmstadt in 1831. His father brought him to St. Louis in 1840, five years after his mother's death. He went to St. Mary's Parish School and then worked at Roher's Business College on Fourth Street near Pine. He entered the stove and tinware business at 1722 South Broadway. He was elected city treasurer in 1872 and served two terms. He was a Democrat in politics and active in Catholic circles, a member of the St. Vincent de Paul Society, on the board of the German St. Vincent's Orphans Home, and an active member of Sts. Peter and Paul Parish.

Peter G. Gerhart, of Alsatian background, was born in Baltimore. He came to St. Louis, entered real estate, married Octavia Flandrin from one of the French colonial families, and was a member of the city council.

Another large family of Westphalians, the Griesediecks, boasted several prominent members of the brewing industry. One of them, Henry Griesedieck, Jr., came with his parents to St. Louis in 1870 at the age of sixteen. He took two terms at Jones Business College, learning bookkeeping and improving his English. During this time, young Henry worked at Lafayette Brewery, partly owned by his uncle, Frank Griesedieck. With two brothers, Bernhart and Joseph, who had studied brewing in Bavaria, Henry bought the Stumpf Brewery on Nineteenth and Shenandoah Streets. In 1891 Henry and his brothers erected the National Brewery at Eighteenth and Gratiot Streets. This brewery remained in the family until 1907, when it became a constituent of the Independent Breweries Company. Henry accepted the presidency.

Henry and his wife Rosa Grone had five sons and a daughter. Their daughter Frances attended the Sacred Heart Academy at Maryville. Their sons Anton, August, Raymond, Edward, and Robert attended Saint Louis University. Their other son Henry Ernst attended St. Stanislaus (later Quincy) College. The family resided in Compton Heights and worshipped at St. Francis de Sales Church.

Jacob Gross was head of one of the most famous merchandising companies in the Rocky Mountain region. He was educated by the Christian Brothers. His grandfather came from Alsace, and his grandmother was the daughter of an Irish revolutionary. He himself married the youngest daughter of Moses Linton. Their descendants have been very active in St. Louis. His brother was the Most Reverend William Gross, archbishop of Portland, Oregon, who blessed the cornerstone at the second St. Francis Xavier Church on Grand at Lindell.

Frederick Heim, a Tyrolese, came to St. Louis in 1850, opened a lumberyard at Fourteenth and Russell, and prospered. He served in the Home Guards during the Civil War, along with his three brothers. He was a member of the Catholic Knights, independent in politics, but strongly Catholic in religion. He was a business associate of Francis Saler, mentioned several times already.

Alois Helmbacher, an iron manufacturer, born in Alsace in 1829, came to St. Louis with his father, also an iron-master, in 1861. He forged iron for the Eads gunboats that General Grant used to open the Mississippi during the Civil War. He bought stock in the Lafayette Bank and the newspaper *Amerika*. He took an active part in the work of the St. Vincent de Paul Society. His son Michael became a priest in the archdiocese. Alois later joined with two of his brothers, Michael and Peter, in the Helmbacher Forge and Rolling Mill Company.

Francis D. Hirschberg, born in 1854 in St. Louis, gained prominence in Western insurance circles. His father came from Rhenish Bavaria and affiliated with a steamboat lines and a number of other business interests. His mother, Lucille Chauvin, was of a French colonial family. He married Mary Frost, a daughter of General Daniel M. Frost, and moved in top social circles. He served on the board of consultants to Father William Banks Rogers, President of Saint Louis University. He and his wife were liberal contributors to church and charity.

Bernard Israel, a manufacturer and broker, was born in Westphalia in 1814. The son of a cooper, Bernard became a journeyman cooper in Cincinnati in 1848. He came to St. Louis several years later and, in partnership with his brother, established a cooperage business. They manufactured pork barrels, especially useful during the Civil War in feeding the Union troops. He entered the banking business late in life, was a judicious investor, and left a fortune. A Democrat and Catholic, he gave property to the Little Sisters of the Poor and to the St. Vincent's Orphans' Home.

Herman Kriegshauser, a skilled woodworker, came to St. Louis from Germany with his brother Adam in 1850, opened a furniture store on the near Northside, and in 1879 made furniture at his shop on Ninth Street. Later, the family enterprise moved to Manchester Road at Sarah Street. In 1891, George and Rose Kriegshauser opened a funeral parlor. Several members of the Kriegshauser family have been involved in funeral direction ever since, currently serving from locations at Kingshighway just south of Chippewa and on Olive Boulevard, a few blocks west of I–170.

Henry Niemeyer was born in 1817 in Hanover. He was a Republican and a devout Catholic. He was involved in steamboats and then in street paving. He was the owner of a large stone quarry in Keyser's Hill, Missouri, and eventually became a wealthy contractor and builder.

Four more Westphalians chose St. Louis. Heinrich and Gerhart Venverloh were coopers, possessing a skill needed by the many breweries in the city. Peter Oberemeier, a successful banker, aided educational, religious, and charitable enterprises. Philip Pollhans began making clocks. He moved the business to 1834 Hogan Street, adjacent to St. Liborius Church. Over the years the Pollhans and descendant George Hoffman built clocks for many churches: Holy Trinity, Holy Cross, All Saints, St. Joseph's, and others. With pocket watches costly at that time, many parishioners guided their day by the clock in the church steeple. Each evening little Augie and Hilda had to be at their places at the table before the sixth chime.

Julius Peterson, from Flensburg on the Danish border and a convert member of St. Joseph's Parish, founded the prosperous seed company that bore his name. A director of Lafayette Savings Company, he outlived all other directors. In 1901 his son Julius, Jr., followed his father as treasurer of the Julius Peterson Commission Company.

Henry Ratermann, a cabinetmaker from Ankum in Hanover, came to St. Louis in 1866. In 1873 he entered into a contracting partnership. Twenty years later, he

Left: Hanging Case Clock, built by Adam Pollhans as a wedding gift for his wife.
Right: Mechanism of a Pollhans Clock, originally installed at Sts. Peter and Paul.

dissolved the partnership and established the Ratermann Building and Contracting Company. He constructed many buildings within the Catholic community. His best-known structure was the "Tyrolean Alps" at the 1904 World's Fair, one of the largest and most artistic concessions at the exposition.

William Schotten, a merchant and manufacturer, born in Westphalia in 1819, was educated in parochial schools there. In 1847 he came to St. Louis because many Germans were locating in the Mound City. He opened a spice factory on Walnut, across from the Cathedral. Soon he was doing $200,000 of business annually. His son Hubertus carried on the business and gave liberally to the Church. Edward Vogt, father of eight, landscaped many Catholic institutions.

John Winkelmann, a shoemaker by trade, left Lammersheim, Bavaria, in 1866, at the age of sixteen. Settling in Carondelet, he married Paulina Louis at St. Boniface Church in 1871. Their two oldest sons, Ernest and Henry, became pharmacists, starting a family tradition. Eventually ten Winkelmann drug stores dotted the map of St. Louis. A grandson, Ernest, was president of the Catholic Union of Missouri and a pioneer in the Laymen's Retreat League. A cousin, Christian, was the first St. Louis–born bishop of Germanic ancestry.

Numerous others left their imprint.

Top: The Very Reverend Christian Winkelmann, first local bishop of German ancestry on the day of his first mass.
Bottom: Father Servatius Altmicks, O.F.M., meets with thirteen of the original fifty local members of the Third Order of St. Francis, at the Franciscan Friary on Meramec St. in 1863.

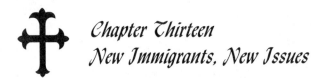

Chapter Thirteen
New Immigrants, New Issues

While immigration slackened during the Civil War, the unification of Germany under militaristic Prussia and the anti-Catholic laws of Chancellor Otto von Bismarck drove many people, lay and clerical, from Germany to St. Louis. While local German Catholics, long-established and recent arrivals, had no connection with the Kaiser's Empire, they cherished the language, literature, and music of the "Old Country," as they came to call it.

Two Southside parishes had opened earlier: St. Agatha's on South Ninth Street at Utah, in the area of the large breweries, and St. Francis de Sales on Ohio near Gravois. After several years in small, temporary church buildings, each parish then planned a more permanent structure.

The first St. Agatha's parish building was a two-story combination of church and school. The congregation built a red-brick church in 1884 and enlarged it in 1899. German-trained Adolphus Druiding drew up plans for both efforts. St. Louis architect Joseph Stauder served as contractor for the second church. The firm of Dierkes and Hoogstret provided the brickwork and that of Erbs and Rieth, the stonework. Max Schneiderhahn and A. T. Kaletta gave several statues. In 1905 Emil Frei installed fourteen new windows.

St. Francis de Sales Parish, called an "ambitious daughter" of Sts. Peter and Paul, was eventually to succeed the latter as the main German parish in St. Louis. In 1894 the pastor, Father Peter J. Lotz, set out to build "the largest and finest church in the city," certainly an ambitious goal. Many setbacks slowed progress, especially the tornado of 1896, which destroyed the earlier church but left the school intact. The church was not completed until the new century under the leadership of parishioner-architect Viktor Klutho. Wagener Brothers did the brickwork, Emil Frei crafted the art glass, and Max Schneiderhahn made the sculptures. The single tower soon dominated the South City skyline.

Above: St. Francis DeSales took the leadership among German parishes. Bishop Christian Winkelmann was pastor in the 1930s.

Left: Emil Frei, Sr., expert in art glass.

The archdiocese continued to open parishes for German worshipers: St. Aloysius in 1872, in the southwest section of the city; Perpetual Help, far to the north, in 1873; St. Augustine on the near Northside; St. Bernard, straight west at Rock Springs, in 1874; St. Henry's, west of Jefferson, a few blocks south of Chouteau, in 1885; and St. Engelbert's at Marcus and Carter in 1891. Holy Ghost (1909) and St. Barbara's (1893) located in the Central West. St. Aloysius and St. Engelbert's had unique histories.

St. Aloysius opened in 1872 in a unique way. German Catholics living beyond present-day Sublette Park in the southwest section of the city petitioned Vicar-General Muehlsiepen for clearance to organize a parish. Sixty families were willing to cooperate and contributed. They bought ten acres on Reber Place for $8,500, laid out three blocks, and reserved the middle one for a church. The promoters sought Catholics from other Southside parishes, such as St. Bernard and Sts. Peter and Paul.

The Reverend Frederick G. Holweck became pastor. A frame church went up, dedicated to St. Aloysius. The School Sisters of Notre Dame immediately opened up a school. Soon 130 families formed the flock. At that time, Italians from the area of Milan sought jobs in the clay pits a few blocks north of St. Aloysius Parish. Monsi-

Right: St. Aloysius on Reber Place in southwest St. Louis.

gnor Holweck, fluent in Italian, invited them to worship at a ground-level chapel he reserved for them until Monsignor Caesar Spigardi organized St. Ambrose Parish.[1] After laboring for many years in northeastern and southeastern Missouri, Father Francis Brand shepherded the St. Aloysius flock well into the twentieth century. Even after World War I, he preached in German at one Mass every Sunday.

Typical of the people coming to St. Aloysius, the Hanneke Brothers came from Germany and took residence in the parish. Ignatius, born on the boat coming from the old country, ran an independent packing house from his home and a hardware store on the southeast corner of Southwest Avenue (then called "Old Manchester Road") at Macklind Avenue. His brother opened a pharmacy across the street. With twenty sons between them, the two brothers saw their families grow and expand into other parishes. Ignatius built the family residence on Arsenal Street in Epiphany Parish. A grandson, Richard Hanneke, became a priest of the archdiocese.

Expansion of the city to the northwest matched that to the southwest. Catholics living to the south and west of Bellefontaine and Calvary Cemeteries needed a church. With Vicar-General Muehlsiepen present, the parishoners-to-be met at the home of Engelbert Schapers on March 30, 1891. One present was Arnold Steinlage, who had sold the property on Shreve at Carter to the organizers. Among them were Rademachers, Poelkers, Dreyers, Kissells, Goelners, Braumschwigs, Schaefers, and Jacobsmeyers, names to surface regularly in Catholic circles over the years.

The archbishop approved their plans. Father Muehlsiepen designated Father Anton Pauck pastor of St. Engelbert's. The new pastor displayed a valuable gift for fostering vocations and promoting parish organizations. The parish soon had a flourishing unit of the Sodality, the Catholic Knights of America, the St. Vincent de Paul Society, the Western Catholic Union, the German St. Vincent's Orphans Society, and others. School Sisters of Notre Dame taught large classes at the school. Twelve girls of the parish joined the School Sisters in the first fifty years, and six went to other congregations. Six young men became priests over the years.

In the meantime, German socialists gained control of some labor unions, especially in the brewing industry. At the start of the Civil War, sixty shopkeepers had brewed lager. Gradually four large firms produced the bulk of the product. The socialist workers took the same anticlerical position as the Forty-Eighters of an earlier decade. All brewery workers had to subscribe to a socialist paper. Some unions had their headquarters at a *Turn Verein*, the regular rendezvous of the Forty-Eighters.

The German-Catholic workers were suspicious of such labor leadership, and also of the Knights of Labor, but for different reasons. Terence Powderley, the president of this first big labor union, was an Irish Catholic, but the union had certain fraternal ceremonies that seemed to suggest it was a secret society of the type condemned by Rome. This was later clarified, but by that time the Knights had passed their peak. Eventually, numerous German-Catholic workers joined the American Federation of Labor.

In Cologne, Germany, in the meantime, a priest of that archdiocese, Father Adolf Kolping, began a socioreligious organization for young men working in large cities. In those days in Europe, socialism made great strides in winning recruits for their labor organizations, especially among workers newly coming from the farming areas. Immigrant workers brought the Catholic Kolping Society to St. Louis in 1856. It was the first unit in America.

The last quarter of the century saw an amazing growth of the Catholic Knights of America, especially among German-Catholic congregations in the city of St. Louis. This soundly established fraternal insurance society set up thirty-four branches, with 2,819 members in St. Louis. The organization grew extensively until the later-forming Knights of Columbus gradually overshadowed it. But the Catholic Knights kept on and ultimately set up their headquarters in St. Louis. It continued strong in such German-background parishes as St. Joseph, Holy Trinity, St. Liborius, and Our Lady of Perpetual Help.

During the last decades of the nineteenth century, religious orders and congregations whose members had come from one country of Europe—the Vincentians from Italy, the Sisters of St. Joseph and Religious of the Sacred Heart from France, and the Sisters of Mercy and the Christian Brothers from Ireland—began to welcome candidates of Germanic background.

Notable was the Missouri Province of the Jesuit Order. Originally mostly Belgian in personnel, it gradually expanded to include many nationalities. Among those of German background, Francis H. Stuntebeck headed Saint Louis University immediately following the Civil War. Three other German Jesuits held that post during the remainder of the century. The most noted of them, Father Joseph Keller, grew up in St. Louis. After serving as president of the university, he headed Woodstock College in Maryland, the theology school for Jesuits of the entire country. Eventually, he rose to be the assistant to the superior general for English-speaking countries. Father Rudolph J. Meyer grew up near Tower Grove Park and led the Missouri Jesuits as provincial for two non-consecutive terms. Father John P. Frieden, a Luxembourger, had a brilliant term as Saint Louis University president (1908–1911) that was cut short by his early death.

The Christian Brothers had come from Ireland before the Civil War, welcomed many excellent candidates, and in a few years, were teaching at Christian Brothers College, two academies, and in ten parish schools in St. Louis. In the 1880s, the College moved to a northwest city location at Kingshighway and Easton. While few Christian Brothers were German, many candidates for the clergy of Germanic ancestry took their basic Latin from the brothers. Among them were the Most Reverend James Schwebeck, D.D., bishop of La Crosse, Wisconsin, three Vincentians—Herman Menningers, Francis Moser, and Justin Nulle—Redemptorist John Keyser, and Passionist Paul Jokerst.

Early in the twentieth century, Brother Baldwin (born Leopold Witzleben) headed Christian Brothers College. During those same years, the CBC championship soccer team listed several Cessmans, a Feisel, and a Reichsteigen amid the Raticans and Branigans. None, however, challenged Harry Ratican as the top player of the country in those days.

The Marianists began their ministry in St. Louis with a boys' school at Sts. Peter and Paul Parish during the Provincialate of Father George Meyer. Brother George Kaiser began classes in 1898. The congregation set up a lay school and a house of formation at Chaminade College on Denny Road (later Lindbergh Boulevard) in St. Louis County, and a distinct province in 1910. Eventually, the Marianists developed a seminary program at Maryhurst Normal in southwest St. Louis County. Brother John Waldron, an architect, supervised the Marianist buildings. In 1913 they opened Kenrick High School near St. Bridget's Church on the Northside, under the direction of Brother Gerald Mueller.

When Coadjutor Archbishop Patrick J. Ryan left for Philadelphia in 1884, Archbishop Kenrick named Father Philip P. Brady to take his place as vicar general for English-speaking parishes. A priest of average natural gifts, he faced a position that called for another Patrick Ryan.

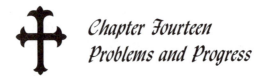

Chapter Fourteen
Problems and Progress

Stories of tiffs between the Irish and the Germans abound in local folklore. Interesting as they are, they left no solid evidence of their happening. The first attacks the Germans faced came not from the Irish but from Anglo-American, anti-immigrant "Know Nothings." The Catholic Irish and church-going Protestant immigrants were also targets of these nativists. History is clearly aware of these.

Before the city organized its fire department, men's clubs fought fires. They also fought rival teams for the right to fight a particular fire. Some clubs were totally Irish. These fights had no Irish-German aspect. Over the years, athletic contests ended in fisticuffs. On occasion they might have been Irish-German, but they might likewise have involved English, Scotch, Poles, Italians, and others.

Sometimes a fine line separated Irish and German neighborhoods on the Northside. At one time, Fourteenth Street was the dividing line. When a young boy of German ancestry told his father that he'd never cross Fourteenth Street, his father scolded him: "Are you afraid of an Irish boy?"

"Not of one, Father," he replied, "but of five."

Apparently the Irish had a well-defended line.

The last memorable fisticuffs in the southwest section of the city took place in Clifton Heights Park. It grew out of a softball game between the teams from playgrounds in the area. A few participants on one side may have been Irish or German. The rival leaders were neither.

Evidence suggests that these alleged Irish-German brawls made good copy for newspapers, far beyond their actual significance.

This chapter could cite examples of German-Irish cooperation and sharing. Two parishes in Carondelet, St. Columcille (Irish) and St. Boniface (German) united in an annual Corpus Christi procession. As the years went on, a military band from Jefferson Barracks added a little more color and a lot more music. Men of St. Patrick's and St. John's took part in cornerstone layings, jubilees, and other ceremonies at Sts. Peter and Paul and other Southside churches. Men of St. Henry's and St. Liborius marched in the long procession the day of the cornerstone laying at the new St. Francis Xavier Church on Grand at Lindell. Archbishop William Hickey Gross, C.SS.R. of Portland, Oregon, preached.

The only public confrontation between Irish and German Catholics stemmed from a pastor's surprising action during the Franco-Prussian War (1870–1871). To the dismay of Irish worshippers, and no doubt of many Germans also, the otherwise popular pastor, Father Peter Wigger, offered prayers for the success of the Prussian Army in its war against France. Led by prominent businessman Edward Dowling, the Irish immediately left Holy Cross and appealed to Archbishop Kenrick, who set up a new parish farther north, Our Lady of Mount Carmel, for non-Germans in Baden.

When the German states joined together to fight the French in 1870, the "Forty-Eighters" in St. Louis had to choose between unity and liberty. They chose unity. They enjoyed the support of the English-language press that preferred the German Kaiser to the French Emperor Napoleon III. The Germans won and united under Kaiser Wilhelm I of Prussia. Many German groups in St. Louis joined together in public celebration in honor of the new German Empire. Any warmth the average German Catholic had for the new empire, however, ended shortly when Chancellor Otto von Bismarck began a decade-long persecution of Catholics.

Bismarck's laws against Catholics in the 1870s provoked a fresh surge of emigration to St. Louis from Paderborn in the eastern section of Westphalia. Among these were Sisters of Christian Charity, founded in Paderborn by Mother Magdalen von Mallinckrodt. They took charge of St. Vincent's Home and opened schools at St. Bernard's, St. Augustine's, and Resurrection.

Among lay folk from Paderborn, the Vorbecks had anticipated the Bismarckian persecution. Two sons and three daughters of Judochus Vorbeck and his wife Anna Maria had come to the States. Joseph Vorbeck settled in St. Joseph's Parish and became a citizen in 1855. He apprenticed as an engineer on the short run from the clay pits in Cheltenham to the kilns and eventually won a regular run on the Frisco.

In the meantime, his brother Herman, who had tilled a farm near Aurora, Illinois, followed him to St. Louis in 1864. Three of their sisters and their husbands did likewise: Catharena Kaup and her husband Herman; Catherina Kroeger with her husband John, and Margaret Stickling and her husband Henry.

Among the many descendents of the Vorbecks were two Jesuit priests, Fathers Joseph Kroeger and Herman J. Pickert, and three nuns, Sister Mary Erasma and Sister M. Theodine, School Sisters of Notre Dame, and Sister Maria Assumta, a Lorretine.

Chancellor von Bismarck also drove Catholic businesses to seek addresses elsewhere. Among these, he forced Herder, Inc., a distinguished international publishing house owned by the Herder family in Freibourg, Germany, to look for publishing and distribution centers elsewhere in the world. Among the five they chose, St. Louis was the only one in the New World. But before we go into its coming to St. Louis, a look at this distinguished firm in Catholic publishing is in order.

Bartholomew Herder founded the firm in 1801. His sons Carl Raphael and Benjamin joined him. The older, Carl Raphael, handled business matters. The younger, Benjamin, expanded the scope of the publishing to include scholarly works in general. He ultimately published a five-volume *Catholic Encyclopedia* and hoped eventually to set up a theology center.

Historian William Linz wrote of him in the *New Catholic Encyclopedia*: "Because of his farflung and varied publishing programs, Benjamin Herder was a major influence in the Catholic revival of nineteenth-century Germany."[1] His son and successor, Herman (1864–1937), brought out papal encyclicals and initiated the publishing of Ludwig von Pastor's *History of the Popes*. As mentioned earlier, he set up an international network of publishing and distribution divisions in Vienna, Rome, Barcelona, Tokyo, and St. Louis. The choice of St. Louis over all cities in the New World strengthens a central theme of this book, namely, that in the mid-nineteenth century, St. Louisans could boast that theirs was the best German-Catholic community in America.

From 1873 to 1899, Herder's St. Louis office distributed books published in Europe. After the turn of the century, however, it shared the publishing program.

Above: William Dehne led the German parishioners, who marched to St. Francis Xavier Church to hear Archbishop William Gross of Portland, Oregon, speak at the laying of the cornerstone on Trinity Sunday, June 8, 1884.

✝ Chapter Fifteen
Catholics in Controversy

A controversy arose between the Catholics who wanted speedy assimilation and those advocating gradual progress. Archbishop John Ireland of St. Paul, Minnesota, led one group, and Archbishop Michael A. Corrigan of New York the other. The German Catholics favored the latter party. They saw assimilation as inevitable, of course, but as a slow and natural process. They looked on the preservation of language and customs in the national churches as a sure way of preserving the faith. They sided with the English-speaking conservatives who pointed to the obvious Protestantism and the periodic nativism of Anglo-Americans that was to erupt again in the early 1890s with the American Protective Association.

Archbishop Ireland hoped to keep parochial schools within the mainstream of public education and was trying to find a workable program of cooperation in the two Minnesota towns of Fairbault and Stillwater. St. Louisan Father David Phelan, editor of the *Western Watchman*, strongly supported Archbishop Ireland's position on the parochial schools. He felt they were islands of foreignism rather than American institutions. His brother Michael, a state legislator and business manager of the *Western Watchman*, worked with Senator Henry Spaunhorst in the Missouri legislature to win a just distribution of state funds in education. The Constitution of Missouri, however, drawn up by anti-Lincoln Republicans in 1866, outlawed reasonable cooperation. In the meantime, too, Archbishop Ireland's attempts to work with the public school system were facing rebuffs.

On the German side in St. Louis, Father Francis Goller of Sts. Peter and Paul Parish had vigorously advocated parochial schools nationally. The Third Plenary Council of Baltimore in 1884 strongly urged the spread of parish schools. It said nothing, however, about another issue in the St. Louis German-Catholic community: the status of the non-English speaking churches like St. Mary's of the Victories and St. Joseph's that lacked full parochial recognition. At the council, Vicar-General

Above: Girls of St. Anthony's kindergarten with their dolls.

Muehlsiepen had sought clarification of this issue.

In 1886 Father Peter M. Abbelen, vicar-general of the Milwaukee diocese, carried a petition to Rome that asked for a resolution of this issue and discussed, in general, the relationship of Irish Catholics and German Catholics in the United States. One matter of complaint was the obvious disproportion between bishops of Irish ancestry and those of German ancestry. The entire Abbelen affair stirred up, rather than calmed, the growing Irish-German controversy.

In February 1887, sixty-five German-speaking priests from various dioceses gathered in Chicago for the first meeting of a newly forming German-American Priests Society. Under the chairmanship of St. Louis's Vicar-General Muehlsiepen, the conferees planned a huge meeting of German Americans to be held the following September in Chicago at the time of the *Central Verein* congress. Further, Muehlsiepen proposed a collection for a temporary residence and orientation center in New York for newly arriving German Catholics, to be called Leo House in honor of Pope Leo XIII. The collection succeeded in accomplishing this goal.

The second meeting of the German-American Priests Society in 1889 called for mutual cooperation with other groups. It proved difficult to win Archbishop Ireland and his supporters over to this annual united manifestation of Catholic faith. At the time, Archbishop Ireland rejected the leader of Ruthenian Catholics. Their descendants make up a majority of the congregations of Orthodox churches in America today.

In 1891 a meeting of representatives of various societies that helped immigrants met in Lucerne, Switzerland. Unfortunately, the United States had no representative. The delegates made two major recommendations for dealing with Catholic immigrants: separate churches and schools for each nationality, and clergy who spoke the respective languages. The delegates thought it desirable, further, to have representatives of each national group in the episcopacy. In itself, the document was harmless, but false reports of it came to the United States from an Americanist agent in Rome, which proved disastrous for the German-Americans. Historian Gerald P. Fogarty, S.J., documents this aspect of American history. He shows that the agent, Father Denis J. O'Connell, magnified and sometimes falsified the German-American proposals.[1]

A series of telegrams attributed the Lucerne memorial to the German nationals alone, even though six other nationalities had taken part. These telegrams misquoted the moving spirit behind memorial, the zealous German layman Peter Paul Cahensly, and accused him of working in the interests of the German Empire. Actually, he belonged to the Central Party, which opposed most of Chancellor von Bismarck's policies, including his anti-Catholic laws.

One charge claimed that the priests in St. Louis had brought about the Lucerne meeting and had made various requests there. In an article in the St. Louis paper *Westliche Post*, Cahensly denied that the memorial had originated in St. Louis and that the Central Party in the German legislature had sponsored it. Nonetheless, some Catholics accepted these false charges. At this time, Cahensly made a true but undiplomatic statement. He said, "It is a well known fact that the Irish in America try to obtain all the bishoprics possible for themselves."[2] Even though more German priests than Irish priests worked in St. Louis after the Civil War, Bishop Joseph Melcher of Green Bay was the only St. Louis priest of German ancestry raised to the episcopacy, while eight born in Ireland went from St. Louis to guide other dioceses during Kenrick's half-century. In fact, St. Louis priests shepherded half of America's Catholics in 1890. Cahensly had spoken the truth, but the reaction was bitter.[3]

Archbishop Ireland blamed all the troubles on "the clique of foreign-minded and short-sighted Catholics of St. Louis."[4] A supporter of Archbishop Ireland, Father John Conway, singled out as tireless workers in the cause of foreignism the Very Reverend Henry Muehlsiepen and the Reverend William Faerber of St. Louis—and he called the entire effort a conspiracy against the country.[5] Aging Archbishop Kenrick failed to defend these two great priests of the archdiocese whose loyalty to their adopted country was so brutally questioned.

The backlash against the Lucerne memorial identified the German Catholics with the Bismarck Empire that had expelled many of them and put all German-Catholic leaders on the defensive at the turn of the century. But the everyday German Catholics at St. Anthony's or Holy Trinity went their steady ways undisturbed by the high-level discussion.

By the time of Archbishop Kenrick's Golden Jubilee as a bishop, it was clear that the old "Lion of the West," as many called him, could well rest in his den. He asked that Father Philip Brady, vicar-general for English-speaking parishes, be named his coadjutor with right of succession. The pastors of the city met at Father Ziegler's rectory and drew up their own list in a letter to Cardinal Gibbons of Baltimore. Bishop John J. Kain of Wheeling, West Virginia, held the top slot. Father Brady did not make the *terna* countdown, the required list of three. While two Irish pastors refused to sign the letter, all foreign-language pastors did.

Bishop Kain came to St. Louis in 1893 as apostolic administrator and coadjutor. But no one, apparently, had properly notified Archbishop Kenrick. For several months confusion snarled ecclestiastical traffic. The German Catholics were not immediately involved. The affair was totally an Irish donnybrook on a high level.

✝ Chapter Sixteen
German-Catholic Press

German Catholics in St. Louis published extensively over the years. By 1910, they put out one daily paper, five weeklies and semi-weeklies, one fortnightly, and two monthly magazines. This gradual development began with Father Martin Seisl's editing of the weekly *Herold des Glaubens* (*The Herald of the Faith*) in 1850. His work came up early in this account in the discussion of prominent pastors of St. Joseph's Church. The firm of Blattau and Kessel was its first publisher. From 1851 to 1875, Francis Saler published a daily paper, *Tages-Chronik* (*The Daily Chronicle*).

Vicar-General Henry Muehlsiepen began the *Pastoral-Blatt* (*Pastoral Pages*), a monthly for Catholic clergy throughout the nation. Father William Faerber edited it until his death. Later, B. Herder, 17 South Broadway, issued the magazine and published theological treatises, thus gradually widening its readership.

During the period of Chancellor Otto von Bismarck's persecution of Catholics that followed the unification of Germany under Prussia in 1871, the local secular German press showed a sharply anti-Catholic tone. In 1872 the Catholics answered with a daily paper, *Amerika*. G. Helmich was its first editor. Dr. Edward Preuss, once the leading lay Lutheran theologian and a convert to the Catholic Church, edited the paper for thirty years. Upon his death in 1904, his oldest son Arthur stepped in for a short time and invited Frederick Kenkel of Chicago to take over. A corporation styled the German Literary Society, under the presidency of Joseph Gummersbach, head of Herder in St. Louis, sponsored the paper. John Pitzmeier handled business matters for thirty years.

Arthur Preuss had founded a semimonthly, the *Fortnightly Review*, an English-language magazine, in Chicago in 1895. The next year he moved to St. Louis. He strongly supported the papal encyclical *Testem Benevolentiae* of January 22, 1899, even though Archbishop John J. Kain, successor to Kenrick, and most liberal bishops had their misgivings. Conservative prelates like Archbishop Michael A. Corrigan of New

Left: Dr. Edward Preuss (1834–1904), theologian, convert, controversialist.

York and Bishop Bernard J. McQuaid of Rochester welcomed Pope Leo XIII's message.

The papal letter condemned a set of attitudes called "Americanism." This term surfaced in response to a review in French of a life of Father Isaac Hecker, founder of the Paulist Fathers. The review brought strong responses, both approving and condemning. At least the term was unfortunate in that what the encyclical meant by "Americanism" differed from what Americans understood the term to mean.

Arthur Preuss in St. Louis reprinted articles that saw the encyclical as a justified and paternal warning to the Catholics of the United States, especially in stressing natural virtues over the supernatural. In his *Fortnightly Review*, then, he took the side of the conservative archbishops against his own Archbishop John J. Kain, who denied that the enumerated heresies existed in this country. Preuss was criticized in many circles for his position, but he still received high commendation for his services to religion from Archbishop Joseph Satoli, the apostolic delegate, and continued to publish his *Fortnightly Review* well into the twentieth century.

In 1900 Clement Willenbrink took over the editorship of *The Herald of the Faith*, with Father Frederick G. Holweck and J. F. Meifuss as co-editors and Louis Blankenmeyer as business manager. Joseph Gummersbach was president of the Board of Directors. Among other writers in the German community at that time, Father Holweck contributed fifty articles related to devotional matters and prerogatives of Our Lady to the *Catholic Encyclopedia*.

Right: Frederick P. Kenkel.

In May 1905, Frederick Kenkel accepted the editorship of the daily *Amerika*, the most influential Catholic German-language newspaper in the United States. Twenty-two years of age but a seasoned journalist of high rating, he had experience in business and management. A devout Catholic and an energetic person, careful in details, with an autocratic tendency, he found difficulty in adjusting to others or in working smoothly with those who differed with him. "Yet his gifts of mind and character," Notre Dame historian Philip Gleason wrote in his book *The Conservative Reformers*, "inspired confidence in his leadership, and he soon became the key figure in the *Central Verein*."[1]

The original *Central Verein* that began in 1855 consisted entirely of local societies serving German-Catholic immigrants and their families. A major structural change was made around 1900. It became a national association of state organizations rather than the previous collection of local societies. The redirected *Central Verein*, eventually to change its name to the Central Bureau, set up headquarters in St. Louis in 1908 with Frederick P. Kenkel as director.[2]

He had not been involved with the controversies that absorbed the German-American Catholics in the 1890s and seems to have had no connection with the Central Bureau until he became editor of *Amerika*. From 1908 onward, his personal career was intimately tied to the organizational life of the German-American Catholics. He was to give the Central Bureau a vision and a mission of social reform that caught the interest of the second generation. In 1912 he was named a Knight of St. Gregory. Under his leadership, the Central Bureau opened St. Elizabeth's Settlement. Principally a day nursery for children of women employed beyond the home, the settlement was staffed by three Notre Dame nuns. Its success stimulated other similar ventures. Kenkel's early years in St. Louis coincided with those of President Theodore Roosevelt's call for social reform.

During those years, Archbishop John J. Glennon, who had succeeded Archbishop Kain, challenged his flock to build a cathedral worthy of the great archdiocese. The people accepted the challenge, and the structure was soon underway at the northwest corner of Lindell Boulevard at Newstead Avenue. The apostolic delegate, Archbishop Diomede Falconio, O.F.M., blessed the cornerstone on October 18, 1908. The drive for this great edifice proved a unifying force. With the cathedral underway, the archdiocese followed with Kenrick Seminary in Shrewsbury, Missouri.

In her book, *St. Louis Germans 1850–1920*, historian Audrey Olson wrote: "By 1914 twenty Catholic parishes with German affiliation" continued in St. Louis. "Catholics accounted for a sizeable portion of the Church-affiliated Germans."[3]

In the meantime, while many Irish parishes welcomed units of the Holy Name Society, German men continued with the men's Sodalities that gave them spiritual vitality.

Chapter Seventeen
Architects and Masters of Art Glass

S hortly after the Civil War, a local architect of Germanic ancestry, Louis Wessbecker, designed churches, among them three for German-speaking parishes,
St. Augustine in 1874, Holy Ghost in 1879, and St. Engelbert in 1891, and
one Polish church, St. Stanislaus in 1882. At that time, St. Louis attracted a number
of German architects, among them priests or members of religious orders. The best
known of these latter was the Franciscan Brother Adrian Wewer, who designed the
churches of St. Francis Solanus at Quincy, Illinois, and St. Anthony of Padua in St.
Louis. Making St. Louis his home base, Brother Wewer traveled across the country to
build monasteries and parish churches. He had no training as an architect but seemed
to have possessed a gift for remembering the structural intricacies of his homeland's
church buildings. After him, two other architects with impeccable credentials, Franz
Georg Himpler and Adolphus Druiding, were able to leave memorable churches in
the American Midwest. They built many Gothic Revival churches for German parishes during the second half of the nineteenth century.

Himpler was born near Trier in Germany in 1833. He studied at the Royal
Academy of Architecture in Berlin between 1854 and 1858. In 1867 he came to
the United States and settled in Atchison, Kansas, where he designed St. Benedict's
Abbey. Between 1873 and 1875 Himpler built his German Gothic masterpiece in
America, Sts. Peter and Paul in St. Louis. He modeled the interior of the church after
the Cathedral of Cologne and the *Liebfrauenkirche* of Trier.

Druiding, a native of Hanover, studied in Berlin and Munich, and coming to the
United States shortly after the Civil War, he settled in St. Louis. He enjoyed wider
success in his career than Himpler, since he was willing to erect modest churches
rather than grandiose temples, which Himpler designed. St. Louis and the Midwest
were ideal locations for Druiding's type. He used red brick, and brick of the best
quality was always available in St. Louis. One of the first churches he built, St. John

Nepomuk, the oldest Bohemian congregation in the United States, was almost completely destroyed in the tornado of 1896. However, the front of the church was not damaged severely and gives an indication of Druiding's original work.

Around the turn of the century, a group of second-generation German-Catholic architects took over, among them Viktor Klutho, who built the great St. Francis de Sales Church in 1907. Klutho also did work outside of St. Louis, such as at the Benedictine Convent church at Ferdinand in southwestern Indiana. In her book *Nineteenth-Century German-American Church Artists* Annemarie Springer concluded, "The city of St. Louis had historically nourished two generations of architects with roots in German ecclesiastical building styles."[1]

In an adjacent field, art glass, Emil Frei excelled. Born in Bavaria in 1869, he studied at the Munich Academy of Art. After a short stay in San Francisco, Frei accepted an invitation to design and install art glass in the new St. Francis Xavier Church on Grand Boulevard at Lindell in St. Louis. The project never came to fruition, but Frei was so taken with St. Louis that he opened his own company at nineteen South Broadway. In 1907 he set up his studio at 3934 South Grand. His wife, Emma Mueller Frei, an immigrant from Heidelberg, assisted him at varying times as secretary, treasurer, and vice-president.

The Emil Frei Company became famous for beautiful stained-glass windows. Frei received many commissions and won a grand prize at the 1904 Louisiana Purchase Exposition in St. Louis. By 1909 the company employed fifteen artists and nine glass-blowers in studios in Munich and St. Louis and, by 1911, had adorned two hundred new churches from New York to San Francisco with figure windows. Frei claimed rightly that the work was equal in every respect to the best imported work.

As his father gradually retired, Emil Frei, Jr., took up and continued with many of the St. Louis churches, among them the pictorial art glass of Jesuit saints at the chapel at St. Stanislaus Novitiate in Florissant. Even though the Jesuits were to withdraw years later, the Gateway College of Evangelism, a Pentecostal group, preserved the windows in the chapel.

In the meantime, the Frei family also had its part in the creation of mosaics in the great Cathedral on Lindell. In conjunction with a Berlin firm, August Wagner, Incorporated, the Freis founded Ravenna Mosaics, Inc., and brought the Heuducks, father Paul and son Arno, experts in installation of mosaic art, to work on the Cathedral. Ravenna would do all the future mosaic work in the great Cathedral of St. Louis and in St. Cecilia's Church near Carondelet Park. Several German artists, among them Professor Felix Baumhauer and Otto Oetken, had their part in the mosaic designs of the Cathedral, but none of them were from St. Louis or located there permanently. Eventually, Ravenna Mosaics, Inc., and the Freis separated. Ravenna continued on South Grand Boulevard. In 1930 Emma Frei retired in favor of her son, Emil, Jr. A thirteen-year veteran of the firm, Julius Gewinner, became secretary-treasurer. Gewinner added the position of vice president after Emil Frei, Sr., died in 1942.

Over the years, Emil Frei, Jr., studied the blue of Chartres Cathedral in France. He entered the building before dawn and watched the effect of the growing sunlight.

Left: Emil Frei, Jr., recaptured the spirit of medieval art glass.
Right: Arno Heuduck installed many mosaics in the New Cathedral.

In his late years, he specialized in one dominating color, usually blue. Among his best works were the transept art glass in St. Francis Xavier College Church, which had brought his father to St. Louis years before.[1] When the visitor looks at those windows, he gazes in awe as he would were he visiting Chartres, Rheims, Cologne, or any of the great cathedrals of Europe.

In 1963, at the death of his father, Emil Frei, Jr., Robert Frei took over the studio, assisted by artist Francis Decke. The firm carried on.

St. Louis Germans excelled in a fourth area of artistry. At the request of young Archbishop Glennon in the fall of 1911, brothers Otto and Emil Mueller set up a shop for the repair, plating, and maintenance of sacred vessels. A few years later, a graduate of Ranken Technical Institiute in St. Louis, Francis X. Kaiser, became an apprentice to the company's founders. From them he learned many of the Old World metal arts techniques used to restore silver and fine metalware, such as hand burnishing, silver casting, smithing, fabrication, and plating. As time went on, Francis married Mary Jo Mueller, a daughter of Otto and Elda Mueller.

In the meantime, Francis' brother, Max S. Kaiser, a graduate of McBride High School, acquired extensive skills in silver restoration, polishing, and highlighting, as well as specialized finishing skills, including applying oxidized, contrasting, bright, satin, and Florentine finishes, and expert plating.

After the retirement of Otto and Emil Mueller in 1947, son-in-law Francis and his brother Max continued the excellent work as Mueller-Kaiser Plating Company. The firm continued to specialize in the skilled restoration of fine church and religious metalware for Catholic, Orthodox, and mainline Protestant churches and Jewish congregations. The company worked with renovation and restoration programs at six Catholic cathedrals in the West and Middle West.

Max Kaiser, Jr., a graduate in history at Saint Louis University, became director of marketing, sales, and liturgical design for Mueller-Kaiser Plating Company.

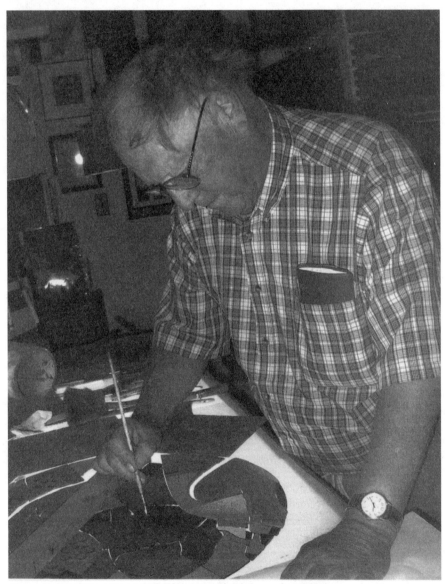

Above: Robert Frei carries on in the footsteps of his father and grandfather.

Chapter Eighteen
Trenches in France, Retrenchment in St. Louis

A recent study of attitudes in Missouri toward the dreadful European War of 1914–1918 shows clearly that the majority of the state looked on our defense perimeter as the Atlantic Coast and not the French rivers, Somme and Marne. The author of this study, Christopher Gibbs, called his book *The Great Silent Minority: Missouri's Resistance to WWI*.[1] Further, countless midwesterners were isolationists who took seriously President George Washington's warning about the danger of entangling ourselves in Europe's endless squabbles. Many St. Louis Irish opposed helping England, though they had a warm feeling for invaded France and a strong dislike of the Kaiser's military machine. In short, they hoped for an Allied victory without our involvement.

Looking at the war as between Germany and England, German Americans favored Germany. But no possibility ever existed for America to enter on Germany's side in the struggle, and no St. Louisans joined the Kaiser's Army. The war was far away.

The internationally known St. Louis editor, William Marion Reedy, had opposed American ventures in the Pacific in the 1890s. Consistently, in 1914, he opposed embroiling ourselves in Europe's latest war. In both houses of Congress, individuals said "No." Congressman William T. Igoe of St. Louis's Northside voted against the declaration of war in 1917. The people re-elected him during the struggle in 1918. At the death of the Austro-Hungarian Emperor, Franz Joseph, in 1916, Archbishop John J. Glennon presided at a memorial Mass at St. Francis de Sales Church for the repose of the soul of the Emperor. Worshippers said prayers in seven languages for the deceased ruler of a nation America was to fight a year later.

While the war in Europe was turning into meaningless slaughter of its youth, the German-American community of St. Louis acted in the interest of future generations. The German St. Vincent's Orphans Home on Hogan Street was overcrowded. The directors of the home found available property for a larger orphanage and extensive parklike grounds at 7401 Florissant Avenue in Normandy. Architect Louis Wessbecker planned the structure, and Ratermann Building and Contracting Company built it. Twenty-three urban parishes with active men's and women's orphans societies took part in the procession at the time of the cornerstone laying on June 26, 1916. The 218 boys and girls moved from Hogan Street to their new home a few months later. Emil Frei art glass adorned the chapel windows. Passionist priests, located in the area, succeeded the Jesuits as spiritual directors.

All the while, the war in Europe grew more intense. America's entrance into the conflict in 1917 brought an all-out effort by the German Army to split the French and British Armies before the full strength of America could hit the Hindenburg Line.

When America declared war, rabble-rousers targeted German Americans in St. Louis.[2] The Catholics suffered along with their ethnic brethren. In the week that Congress declared war, Kenkel received a threatening letter from a writer who identified himself only as "one who knows." He obviously didn't know that Kenkel had two sons in uniform. *Amerika* and other German-Catholic publications had their mail privileges temporarily suspended. St. Louisan Kate Richards O'Hare, the socialist editor of *National Rip-Saw*, as American as President Woodrow Wilson himself, suffered more. The government sentenced her to the federal penitentiary in Atlanta for a remark that the nation was sending Dakota farm boys to be cannon fodder for the Kaiser's guns.

Boys in some neighborhoods of the city began to pelt the trucks of Kaiser-Kuhn Wholesale Grocery with stones. The owners changed the name of the firm to Pioneer Grocer Company. The boys had to find other targets for their throwing arms.[2] In an entirely different area, under the Espionage Act, a local woman turned in her father-in-law who lived with them.[3] He was not deported for disloyalty; instead he found other living quarters to bring domestic peace to one household.

The anti-Catholic paper, *The Menace*, used the opportunity to attack members of the *Central Verein* as a "bunch of traitors and henchmen of the Pope" who deserved deportation to Germany where they could work under the direct supervision of their real bosses, the Pope and the Kaiser. Some of their fellow Catholics protested the use of the German language in sermons. Others used demeaning terms. Editors repeated the false charges of the 1890s that German Catholics had ties with the Kaiser's empire. Westside hostility to the Southside seemed to some analysts to have stemmed from Civil War days.[4]

The German attack failed in the spring of 1918, and the Allies won that fall. But the ideals and hopes of President Wilson faded before the vengeful spirit of powerful European leaders.

Hostilities ceased on November 11, 1918. Two months later, in January 1919, Prohibition became the law of the land, with the ratification of the Eighteenth Amendment to the United States Constitution by the required number of states. The St. Louis Germans and Irish had supported their local congressmen who voted against the amendment—but not for the same reasons. Neither saw drink as evil in itself. Germans looked on wine and beer as integral ingredients of good dining. Among the Irish temperance societies flourished. Their leaders urged those who could not be moderate to pledge to avoid intoxicants entirely. The vote closed the breweries. Beer 'drinkers turned to "home brew," and breweries looked for new products to sell. Temperance societies had to find new approaches.

The war brought about the separate incorporation of the St. Louis branch of Herder's Book Co. The local office kept on publishing under the name B. Herder's and opened a large store of books and religious goods on Broadway in downtown St. Louis. Its most notable publishing venture was an eight-volume work by Charles Augustine, O.S.B., *A Commentary on the New Code of Canon Law*, St. Louis, 1921–1924.

The anti-German prejudice that changed the names of a few streets and several firms and harassed leaders of the German-American community hardly touched the "old neighborhoods."[5] John Walsh still bought coffee cake from Kahlert's Bakery around the corner near Epiphany Church. Neighbors were still neighbors.

People from all over the area still wanted good German food. Herman and Theresa Eisele, immigrants from Munich, opened two popular restaurants, the Bavarian Inn on Arsenal Street near Gravois Avenue and the Black Forest on Michigan Avenue at Cherokee Street. For a time, the Eiseles lived above the Bavarian Inn. Later they moved to Resurrection Parish.

Above: The German St. Vincent's Orphans Home moved to Normandy in 1916.

Chapter Nineteen
The Troubled Twenties

Before the war, America had welcomed immigrants, and the newspapers had featured the customs and costumes of the newcomers. Now the government put quotas on the number of immigrants allowed in each year from individual countries. After the Armistice, newspapers and magazines denounced foreign languages and customs. They ruled out the terms German-American, Irish-American, Polish-American, and other "hyphenated-Americans." Editors stressed the fact that all were Americans. The American population no longer resembled a "salad bowl," but was becoming a "melting pot."

In line with this trend, fifty-five nuns of the Sisters of Mary took out citizenship papers on October 11, 1921. Most of them had come from Germany, but at least one each came from eight other countries. Marguerite Zoff of the Nationalization Office orchestrated the ceremony.

The citywide German organizations, such as the singing societies, disbanded or kept a low profile. The parish societies, among them the Sodalities, Catholic Knights of America, and the branches of the German St. Vincent's Orphans Society, carried on in their quiet, steady way.

The postwar period in America was a time of economic readjustment, over-expansion of farm production, antiunion court decisions, and unemployment. The St. Louis German community, however, did not face the high rate of unemployment that other ethnic groups did, especially the many unskilled African Americans who had moved into St. Louis from the rural South to take menial jobs in wartime. But the general economic uncertainty affected all people. The government had no effective solutions to the many economic problems and no programs for returning veterans.

During those postwar years, Frederick Kenkel revitalized the *Central Verein*. He anglicized the name to the Central Bureau for Social Justice and worked for the benefit of all Catholics, rather than for German-only goals. He published a highly regarded magazine, *The Social Justice Review*. Monsignor John A. Ryan of the Catholic University of America, the leading advocate of social justice among the Catholic priests, praised the journal for its professionalism.[1] Kenkel himself felt that St. Louis was an unusually good place for the Central Bureau. "Our people are loyal to our cause," he stated during hist last days. "Our good priests render all assistance possible."

The Central Bureau began relief programs overseas and at home and promoted institutions of social concerns, such as parish credit unions. St. Andrew's in Lemay led the way, followed by St. Cecilia's and other parishes, mostly of German background. St. Andrew's later joined a consortium of parish credit unions. The seven hundred members of St. Cecilia's Credit Union, led by Treasurer Sheila Harris, felt that the more close-knit parish organization reflected the best interests of the members and could better meet all the purposes of the credit union. The St. Cecilia Credit Union continued to function independently.

A separate Women's Union had formed in the meantime. The two branches generally held joint conventions at both national and state levels. They published news-

Above: Ernest Winkelmann on horseback at the Catholic Union Convention in Herman, Missouri.

papers, assisted immigrants, provided aid to the sick, set up life insurance programs, and showed concern for widows and orphans. Rose Rohman chaired the Women's Union for many years, and Cyril Furrer and Ernest Winkelmann the men's section.

Winkelmann and others at the Central Bureau played an indispensable role in the preparation for the first meeting of the National Catholic Rural Life Committee that took place in St. Louis in 1923. The jubilee history of the organization stressed Kenkel's continuing contribution. A fundamental point of his social thought held that a healthy society required a vigorous middle class. Owners of small productive units of productive property, tradesmen and shopkeepers, as well as farmers, made up Kenkel's "middle class."[2]

Kenkel considered seriously the plight of the family farmer, suffering from the advances of capitalism and large-scale industry, as symptomatic of the danger besetting the middle class as a whole. According to Professor Gleason, "Once a 'veritable yeoman,' and 'the backbone of a virile middle class.' The American farmer in 1929 faced the prospect of degradation to the status of that of a latifundia worker,"[3] that is, a tenant without hope of ever rising to ownership—a peon, such as in Latin America.

So far as agriculture was concerned, leaders of the Central Bureau regarded the cooperative movement as the most hopeful development. Cooperatives not only offered a partial answer to the farmer's immediate problems. They might also prepare the ground for full-scale reconstruction of society.[4]

In his book *A History of the Catholic Church in the United States*," published in 1959 by the University of Notre Dame Press, historian Thomas T. McAvoy, C.S.C., singled out Kenkel as "an ideal Catholic lay leader, exemplary in personal life, able to express his thoughts clearly in good English, and learned in the social problems of the day."[5]

Unfortunately, the country ignored this great concern for widest possible ownership of productive property that so many social reformers felt central to an economically sound nation.

In the post-war years, also, local Catholic historians began to look to their roots and published the first issue of the *St. Louis Catholic Historical Review* in December of 1918. During its five years of existence, it carried articles on the early years of the Church in St. Louis, with the ultimate goal of a history of the archdiocese. The pastor of St. Aloysius Parish, Father Frederick G. Holweck, who had earlier written many articles for the *Catholic Encyclopedia*,[6] evaluated the achievements of pioneer priests of the archdiocese. Monsignor John Rothensteiner had already challenged the pastors of the archdiocese to write the histories of their parishes. In an article in the *Fortnightly Review* for September 15, 1916, he told of the importance of this work, highlighted special features, and insisted on the "whole truth."[7]

In 1917 he published a short history of St. Michael's Parish in Fredericktown, Missouri. As pastor of Holy Ghost Church in St. Louis in the 1920s, he continued to write about various aspects of the early history of the diocese. Ultimately, he undertook the task of writing a two-volume *History of the Archdiocese of St. Louis in Its Various Stages of Development from AD 1673 to AD 1928*, published in 1928. The author detailed the development of institutions in the diocese, parishes, schools, religious congregations, Sodalities, Third Orders, and such. He refrained from comparative analysis of growth in other dioceses or of evaluation of trends in Catholic life. Valuable in itself, his history proved a boon to later historians.

In that same period immediately after World War I, Father Joseph Husslein, a Jesuit who grew up in Milwaukee but spent most of his life at Saint Louis University, put out a book, *Industrial Democracy*, that anticipated the central ideas of Pope Pius XI's encyclical letter of 1931, *Quadragesimo Anno*. Husslein edited many books of Catholic concern under the title "Science and Culture Series," which Bruce Publishing Company published over the years. He also founded the School of Social Science at Saint Louis University. Historian Stephen A. Werner wrote his life story.[8]

Father Michael Gruenthaner, Professor of Scripture at Saint Louis University, wrote for and edited the *Catholic Biblical Quarterly*. Anthropologist Albert Muntsch composed a textbook for college students, *Cultural Anthropology*. Father James Kleist, in cooperation with Father Joseph L. Lilly, C.M., of Kenrick Seminary, published a new translation of the New Testament from the Greek. Lay professors William Korfmacher and Chauncy Finch headed a fine department of classical languages and taught many seminarians as well as lay students. In short, St. Louis writers of Germanic ancestry made distinct contributions to the Church and to the scholarly world of the time.

Herman Kreuger began the *St. Louis Catholic Herald*, a weekly newspaper, in 1921. Especially popular in the German parishes, it gained a wide following throughout the area. Many hoped the archdiocese would accept it officially as the archdiocesan paper. Instead, in 1940, Archbishop Glennon decided to join the *Register* family of newspapers.

In 1925 the twenty-three local and forty-five outstate branches of the German St. Vincent's Orphans Society prepared for its Diamond Jubilee. The members could rejoice in the success of the new orphanage on Florissant Avenue in Normandy. William Bollwerk, Bernard Schulte, John Fehlig, and Henry Wurm made up the main committee for the celebration. The board of trustees at the time included other familiar names: Louis Wessbecker, Edward F. P. Schneiderhahn, Henry Brockland, Carl Gerber, and George Wilmering.

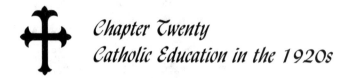

Chapter Twenty
Catholic Education in the 1920s

I n 1922 the Archdiocese of St. Louis opened Rosati-Kain High School, located on Lindell Boulevard at Newstead, directly east of the Cathedral. The school was administered jointly by the School Sisters of Notre Dame, who had developed in a German-Catholic community atmosphere, and the Sisters of St. Joseph, who had developed from a French community to a heavily Irish-American community. It typified the unity of nationalities that had been developing in St. Louis over the years.

The Marianists had begun their St. Louis apostolate in the late nineteenth century by staffing the boys' school at Sts. Peter and Paul Parish. The Society of Mary set up a St. Louis province in 1908, with headquarters in the St. Louis area. The congregation opened Chaminade College on Denny Road (later Lindbergh Boulevard) in suburban St. Louis in 1910. It was a combined boys' boarding school and training school for candidates for the brotherhood. Eventually, the Marianists developed their seminary program at Maryhurst Normal, a few miles south of Chaminade College on Denny Road in Kirkwood. During the early 1920s, the Marianists staffed McBride High School for boys on North Kingshighway, just north of Sherman Park, the former site of Christian Brothers College. Brother John Ringkamp headed the school for many years. The Marianists took charge of Southside Catholic in the next decade.

In the 1910s the Jesuits had staffed four high schools for boys in the area: St. Louis University High School on Grand at Laclede; Gonzaga adjacent to St. Joseph Church on the near Northside; Loyola Academy in the former Eads mansion on South Compton, two blocks north of Lafayette Avenue; and St. Regis at Thirty-fifth Street and Trendly in East St. Louis, Illinois. In 1924 all of these schools were consolidated at St. Louis University High School in a new building, the gift of Mrs. George Backer, on the south side of Oakland Avenue just west of Kingshighway.

After a fire completely destroyed their college on North Kingshighway in 1916, the Christian Brothers concentrated on their high school that opened in 1922 on

Clayton Road at Bellevue.

None of these schools drew their student bodies from only one nationality, as a casual list of their star athletes would indicate: Axtell and Conlon at McBride, Hemp and Curran at St. Louis U. High, Shannon and Stueber at CBC, and McKenna and Stapenhorst at Southside Catholic. St. Francis de Sales, St. Alphonsus, and St. Anthony of Padua Parish had schools for girls. St. John the Baptist Parish had a school for boys and girls that continues at the college preparatory level today. The Lorettines opened Nerinx Hall High School near Webster College in 1924 and closed Loretto Academy on Lafayette Avenue in 1952. The Sisters of St. Joseph, who had arrived in the days of Rosati, primarily to teach deaf children, and had set up their motherhouse in Carondelet, taught at St. Joseph's Academy, St. Anthony of Padua, Rosati-Kain High School, Fontbonne College, and St. Joseph Institute for the Deaf, as well as thirty-four grade schools in St. Louis and St. Louis County. The School Sisters of Notre Dame set up their novitiate and training center along the Mississippi near Jefferson Barracks. They taught at eighteen schools in the city, the same number in the county, and at Rosati-Kain, St. Alphonsus "Rock" High, St. Francis de Sales, and Notre Dame Academy. They, along with the Sisters of St. Joseph, had the largest number of schools in the area at the time of Archbishop Glennon's jubilee in 1928.

Three orders of nuns staffed academies and taught on the grade school level— the Sparkhill Dominicans of New York, the Sisters of Charity of the Incarnate Word, and the BVMs (the Sisters of Charity of the Blessed Virgin Mary). By 1930 few of the schools catered to a distinct ethnic group, one exception being St. Elizabeth's Academy, which seemed to attract a far greater percentage of students with German names than any other.

The religious congregations that had begun with one national group boasted of their expanding range of ancestries. Mother Felicia McGalloway of the Franciscan Sisters of Mary, a congregation from German-speaking lands, directed SSM Cardinal Glennon Children's Hospital. Sister Anna Rose Kraus, an expert in deaf education, spent much of her career at St. Joseph Institute for the Deaf, a school begun by French nuns. William Klemm taught history and coached sports at CBC, a school originally totally Irish in faculty and orientation. Father Henry Hermans was an extremely popular teacher of mathematics at St. Louis University High, a school begun by Belgian Jesuits. Sister Timothy Ryan, S.S.N.D., taught at Notre Dame College adjacent to the motherhouse of the School Sisters of Notre Dame, a once totally German congregation. The college overlooked the Mississippi, just north of Jefferson Barracks.

The roster of religious congregations reflected the "salad bowl" image. For example, from a list selected at random, Gertrude Padberg and Lucy Nordmann joined the Religious of the Sacred Heart; Sisters Ann Bernardine Wackenheim, Rosemarie Groppe, and Mary Philip Bieg joined the Sisters of St. Joseph; Sisters Loyola and Paul Liedel entered the Sisters of Charity of the Incarnate Word; Sister Genevieve Keusenkothen joined the Daughters of Charity; and four Hunleth sisters became Lorettines. Their one brother joined the Jesuits. Their family had been prominent in the music business.

Members of religious congregations in St. Louis had closed ranks and brought together the best of their religious traditions, at the same time opening avenues for those of the many other national groups in the years to come.

GERMAN-AMERICAN CHURCHES 1844–1914

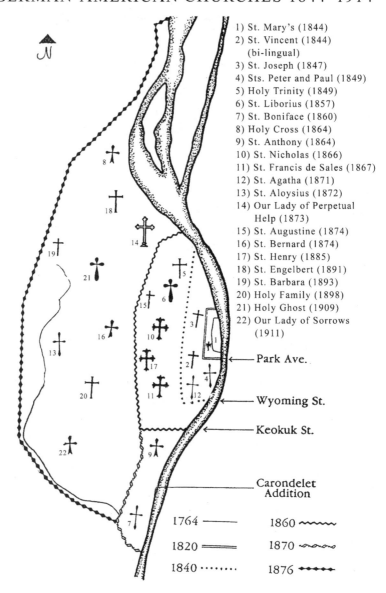

1) St. Mary's (1844)
2) St. Vincent (1844)
   (bi-lingual)
3) St. Joseph (1847)
4) Sts. Peter and Paul (1849)
5) Holy Trinity (1849)
6) St. Liborius (1857)
7) St. Boniface (1860)
8) Holy Cross (1864)
9) St. Anthony (1864)
10) St. Nicholas (1866)
11) St. Francis de Sales (1867)
12) St. Agatha (1871)
13) St. Aloysius (1872)
14) Our Lady of Perpetual
    Help (1873)
15) St. Augustine (1874)
16) St. Bernard (1874)
17) St. Henry (1885)
18) St. Engelbert (1891)
19) St. Barbara (1893)
20) Holy Family (1898)
21) Holy Ghost (1909)
22) Our Lady of Sorrows
    (1911)

← Park Ave.

← Wyoming St.

← Keokuk St.

Carondelet
Addition

1764 ——   1860 ∿∿∿

1820 ══   1870 ᰖᰖᰖ

1840 ·······   1876 ✦✦✦✦

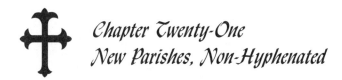

Chapter Twenty-One
New Parishes, Non-Hyphenated

During the 1920s, changes had occurred in the Catholic community. People moving into new parishes, such as Epiphany, were not likely to be of one national background. Earlier churches in that southwestern sector of the city had a distinctly national flavor: Holy Innocents Irish, St. Ambrose Italian, St. Aloysius German. Epiphany, like others on the edge of the city parishes such as St. Luke's and Immaculate Conception in Maplewood, was multinational in ancestry.

While Epiphany's pastor, Father Joseph English, was born in Cork, most parishioners were born in America. Forty percent of the Irish were children of parents who grew up in such parishes as St. Pius V or St. Cronan's. The 40 percent of German background were children of parents who lived in St. Aloysius or Holy Family Parish. The 15 percent Polish came from St. Stanislaus or other downtown parishes, and the few Italians from St. Ambrose or Help of Christians.

When, every March, Father English granted a three-day holiday from St. Patrick's through St. Joseph's Day, people thought of it not as a strictly Irish festival but as a celebration for the entire parish. Bill Hof enjoyed it as much as Mary Alice Dinan, and Leonard Hanneke as much as Marian Sullivan.

The same pattern prevailed in St. Luke's Parish. Bob McFarland lived across the street from Tom Bauer. Mary Hahn selected a home a block away from Frances McDonough. At St. Mary Magdalen on South Kingshighway, Conleys, Niemiras, and Heithauses worshipped.

Parishes that developed within a single nationality welcomed other Catholics. When Monsignor John Rothensteiner, the historian, moved to Holy Ghost on North Taylor at Garfield, the parishioners were mainly of Germanic ancestry. That beautiful church lost several of its windows during a tornado in 1927. Nonetheless, the Irish found it a beautiful place to worship and began to move into the parish.

The 1933 class records at Holy Ghost School listed the following male graduates: Daniel A. Callahan, Paul S. Crowley, John Dolan, Vincent Cross, and George B. Sweeney, who later became state deputy of the Knights of Columbus. On the other hand, there were only three boys of German descent, Elroy Lange, Joseph H. Landolt, and Harold "Pete" Rieser. Sports fans remember Pete Rieser, whose exploits with the Brooklyn Dodgers will come up in a section on star athletes. While so many male graduates in Holy Ghost Parish, once considered a German community, were Irish, all but three of the thirteen female graduates had German names. The total number of students of each heritage was about the same.

With so many new parishes filling up the old limits of the city and jumping to St. Louis County, old national parishes such as St. Lawrence O'Toole matched the map of the Balkans. The pastor bragged of twenty-two distinct nationalities in parochial limits in the postwar years.

All Catholics of the archdiocese looked forward to the dedication of the New Cathedral on Lindell. In his history of the archdiocese, Monsignor John Rothensteiner called the event a "time of spiritual exaltation." The date was June 29, 1926. The timing was excellent since so many distinguished prelates had gathered that summer for a Eucharistic Congress in Chicago. The presence of Patrick Cardinal O'Donnell of Armagh and Michael Cardinal Faulhaber of Munich added luster to the grand festivities in St. Louis.

A short time later, Theresa Backer Kulage, a sister-in-law of Mrs. George (Anna) Backer, who had built a unified Jesuit high school in her husband's memory, prevailed on Archbishop Glennon to invite the Holy Spirit Adoration Sisters (the Pink Sisters) to open a convent in St. Louis. Mother Mary Michael, co-foundress of the contemplative order, accepted the invitation and sent twelve sisters for the first community in St. Louis. Mrs. Kulage donated the property on Adelaide Avenue in North St. Louis just east of O'Fallon Park, situated on the ridge overlooking the Mississippi River. She built and furnished the beautiful chapel at her own expense and financed the construction of the convent. On June 7, 1928, Archbishop Glennon blessed and dedicated the chapel. From then on, one or two sisters have always knelt in prayer before the Blessed Sacrament exposed for veneration.

A magnet, Mount Grace lured many men, women, and children to join the sisters in prayer. Eventually, the men formed the League of a Thousand Men, and later women joined. Federal Highway I-70 opened with a convenient exit on Adelaide Avenue.

In the meantime, the Catholic Knights of America continued its quiet service to its members. Since the fraternal benefit society moved its national office to St. Louis, the spiritual directors were chosen from the St. Louis Archdiocese. One, Monsignor Vincent Naes, pastor of St. Cecilia Church, wrote the history of the Knights, *Rounding Out a Century*. Over the years, Fathers Bernard H. Beeson, Albert J. Bruegger, and Joseph B. Eilers were associate spiritual directors. Fred F. Rottman of St. Louis served a term as national president, and Henry Siemer as national secretary. The national office chose a site on Hampton Avenue as its headquarters.

Above: Liturgy of the Hours at Mount Grace.

Chapter Twenty-Two
The Tentative Thirties

B usiness letdowns—called panics—had hit the country regularly in its history: in 1817, in 1837, in 1857, in 1873, and in 1893. But the Depression that broke out in 1929 had no precedent. The government offered only words, such as "Prosperity is just around the corner." No one had ever seen a corner of that magnitude. Men who had driven Cadillacs to their offices downtown now drove them to Oakland Avenue to mix concrete for the new Walsh Stadium under construction.

The election of Franklin Delano Roosevelt in 1932 first brought hope and then, as far as St. Louis business was concerned, the end of Prohibition and the reopening of the breweries. The late years of the last century had seen the sixty or more small cornerstore breweries give way to the big four—Busch, Lemp, Griesedieck, and Wainwright. In 1920 the Griesediecks bought the Falstaff label from Lemp and called the brewing company the Falstaff Brewing Company. The Falstaff Company moved a major step forward with radio advertising, especially of Cardinals baseball broadcasts. Later, it brought the Cardinals football team from Chicago to St. Louis.

Brewers and pipefitters went back to work. Laws recognized the rights of workers to organize. This proved a boon to the Germans, many of them skilled craftsmen in many phases of construction. The New Deal sponsored public works projects, promoted rural electric cooperatives and other farm programs, and, in general, lessened the visibility of the unemployed. One of the most popular of the Roosevelt programs, the Civilian Conservation Corps, brought young men from cities and towns to the countryside to improve parks and forests. All these helped German Catholics, as they did other Americans.

In the meantime, an Austrian by the name of Adolf Hitler became chancellor of Germany. His ultimate image as a man who did evil was not immediately evident. The first stories from overseas told of improved conditions, the building of roads, and getting people back to work, as had the takeover of Italy by Benito Mussolini in the

1920s. Then Hitler revitalized the German Army allegedly to counteract the Soviet war machine.

The American public responded to Europe's remilitarization with adamant nonintervention. Cartoonists showed "Uncle Sap" not getting involved again. Senator Gerald P. Nye of North Dakota toured the country, telling of his senatorial committee's amazing findings of the manipulation of the munitions makers, often at the expense of their own countries' best interests. The Allies sometimes assisted the Central Powers with needed supplies through neutral countries during the conflict of 1914–1918. One essential munitions plant was in easy range of enemy guns for the duration. But no shell fell on that plant.

Americans, at least those in the Midwest, wanted no further truck with Europe's troubles. When war did break out in 1939, Americans hoped for an Allied victory over Germany without a Soviet domination of Europe, but they had little desire to intervene. Two months before Pearl Harbor, a Senate vote on a draft law to keep in servicemen who had volunteered for a year was 48–48. Only the vote of Vice President Henry Wallace kept those men in uniform.

All the while, on the local religious scene in the 1930s, changes had occurred. The first St. Louis priest of Germanic ancestry to rise to the episcopacy since Bishop Joseph Melcher seventy years before, Monsignor Christian Winkelmann of St. Francis de Sales Parish was consecrated auxiliary to Archbishop Glennon in 1934. Monsignor Paul Schulte, who had written a fine history of the Old Cathedral while pastor there, preceded him in Kansas as bishop of Leavenworth in 1937. Pope Pius XI named Bishop Winkelmann bishop of Wichita two years later. Several priests of German ancestry had wide influence: Monsignor John Tannrath, chancellor of the archdiocese and pastor of the Cathedral on Lindell, and pastors Monsignor Anthony Strauss, Monsignor Bernard Stolte, and Father Victor Suren, a priest of wide interests.

Aloys P. Kaufmann became mayor of the city at the death of his predecessor, William Dee Becker, in a glider accident at Lambert Field in 1943. Joe Darst followed Kaufmann. Later mayors of German ancestry were John Poelker and Vincent Schoemehl.

World War II had no repercussions in the more consolidated St. Louis community comparable to those of World War I. Eichelberger Avenue retained its name and *sauerkraut* was still listed on menus as *sauerkraut*. Nothing of an unusual nature occurred in the old German neighborhoods, as on "The Hill," where a disproportionate number of volunteers overmatched all other neighborhoods in the country.

Far more changes lay ahead for the city, especially in the area of race relations. The only significant action in this area had been the decision of the Sisters of St. Mary of the Third Order of St. Francis to open St. Mary's Infirmary on Papin Street, south of Union Station, to black male patients in March 1933. Within a week, overflow patients from City Hospital No. 2 filled the infirmary. The volunteering sisters were white, nurses and patients black. It was the first step. Sister Clementia Ostoff set the tone.

In 1944 a more significant move occurred. In a sermon to students at Saint

Louis University, the Reverend Claude H. Heithaus, S.J., public relations officer and professor of classical archeology, brought out the moral and ethical issues involved in racial segregation. As a result, the school opened its doors to black applicants in the ensuing term. It was the first university in a former slave state to do so.

In 1945 peace came. Early in 1946, Pope Pius XII named Archbishop Glennon a cardinal of the Church. All St. Louisans rejoiced and decorated Lindell Boulevard for his homecoming. It was not to take place. He died in Ireland on his way back from Rome.

The German Catholics had a great feeling of warmth for Cardinal Glennon. Fundamental to this regard was his magnificent presence and superior oratory. Further, in an interview, Central Bureau leaders praised the cardinal's openness to an unmatched breadth of development.

After the war, the St. Louis office of the Central Bureau became a clearinghouse for relief services, food, medical supplies, and clothing. In its role in the "Displaced Persons" program, the Central Bureau found homes and a livelihood for two thousand immigrants by 1949. The bureau also helped forty-seven Volga-German farmers, refugees from the Soviet Union, find new homesteads in Brazil.

An earlier chapter singled out the Muckermans as typical of the families that grew up in Holy Ghost Parish on the Northside. It centered on the family of Chris Muckerman who supplied the city with ice and coal. All the while, other Muckermans were marrying members of well-known St. Louis families, many of them of German ancestry—Bardenheier, Blumeyer, Bopp, Grone, Hartenbach, Kriegshauser, Schneithorst, Schulte, Switzer, and Wendell. Among these, the Hartenbachs cleaned rugs, the Switzers made candy, and the Schneithorsts ran a popular inn on Lindbergh Boulevard at Clayton Road. Bardenheier retailed wine. As mentioned earlier, the Kriegshausers operated funeral parlors. All these were well-known names throughout the city.

One Muckerman—anthropologist Father Herman Muckerman, a nephew of Chris—taught at Creighton University and returned to Germany shortly before Hitler became chancellor. He fought for freedom of religion in Hitler's Germany. As a result, the officials of Munster named a street in his honor. In more recent years, another priest, Father Norman Muckerman, a Redemptorist, exercised his priestly ministry as a missionary in Brazil and later in religious publishing from the Redemptorist Center at Ligouri, Missouri.

The most widely known of all the Muckermans, Richard, a highly successful businessman, owned the St. Louis Browns. Active in civil and church affairs, he chaired the Archdiocesan Development Drive successfully one year. St. Louis did not really need two baseball teams, just as Boston did not, and both cities lost a team. The Braves went from Boston to Milwaukee, and the Browns went from St. Louis to Baltimore and became the Orioles. Baseball fans in St. Louis still remember that at one time "a Muckerman owned the Browns." Even after the Browns became the Orioles, they kept a few unconquerable supporters like historian William J. Miller and author Bill Borst, who, among other writers, published a book on the team, *Last in the American League: An Informal History of the St. Louis Browns* (1978).

But not all Muckermans, or German Catholics in general, were businessmen or clergymen. Many practiced medicine, among them Doctors Richard Muckerman, Jr., Joseph Keller, Carl Dreyer, Anton Hummel, and Frederick Kistner.

While the Catholics of St. Louis waited for the announcement of their new archbishop, the baseball Cardinals vied with the Brooklyn Dodgers for the National League trophy and the chance to challenge the Boston Red Sox in the World Series for the championship. Among the players, Albert "Red" Schoendiest began his great career at that time. A native of Clinton County, Illinois, he moved to St. Louis and married Mary O'Reilly at St. Margaret's Church. Over the years he played on winning teams in St. Louis and Milwaukee. Later, he managed the Cardinals successfully. From the time the Cardinals won the World Series in 1926, they gradually won the loyalty of the majority of St. Louis.

During those years, other St. Louisans of German ancestry reached the Major Leagues: the already-mentioned Pete Rieser with the Brooklyn Dodgers, "Heine" Mueller with the Cardinals, Don Mueller with the Giants, Emmet Mueller with the Phillies, and Urban Schocker and Herman Schulteheinrich with the St. Louis Browns, among others. While Fred Broeg played football, his brother Bob wrote award-winning sports features for the *Post-Dispatch*, illustrated by Amadee Wohlschlaeger. Broeg also co-authored with Professor William Miller, a St. Louis University historian, the book *Baseball from a Different Angle*. Ray Schmandt starred for the Brooklyn Dodgers

Right: Author Bill Borst, founder of the St. Louis Browns Fan Club.

then returned to his old Northside neighborhood, Bremen, and became an authority on its history. His son Ray, Jr., became a college history professor and wrote textbooks in wide use.

Cecil Muellerlille coached the Billiken football players. The Orf twins played for the Missouri Tigers, along with Paul Christman, who later starred professionally. Bob Stueber and Dick Pfuhl also played in the National Football League. On the high school level, Ralph "Red" Hemp and Vinnie Eberle starred at SLU High, Bob Fuchs and Charley Pons at CBC, and Lou and Ed Drone at McBride.

On the basketball court, too, many names stood out. Among them, Rich Neiman of Du Bourg and St. Louis University, along with Henry Raymonds of SLU High and Dan Miller of McBride. Ed Kohl, a St. Louis University High graduate, and Dick Eckhardt of DeAndreis starred for Regis College in Denver. Bill and Bob Nordmann scintillated at Saint Louis University. George Hasser and Rich Grawer excelled as history teachers and as basketball coaches. Charley Hahn starred in basketball and tennis, Mary Schneidermeyer in tennis, swimming, and figureskating. The "big days" for female athletes came later.

Above: Coach Bob Guelker and the first Billiken NCAA soccer champs (1959).

Top: St. Liborius soccer team on a snowy field.
Bottom: The St. Liborius soccer team could not match St. Leo's eleven.

A major factor in the development of star athletes among St. Louis Catholics was the athletic program of the Catholic Youth Organization. Its director, Bob Guelker, emphasized soccer, long a favorite sport in St. Louis. Soon five thousand Catholic boys and girls were playing the game. Guelker himself coached the Saint Louis University Billikens to five National Collegiate Athletic Association championships.

When Coach Guelker resigned to become head soccer coach and athletic director at Southern Illinois University at Edwardsville, Harry Keough, captain of America's World Cup team in 1950 and successful coach at Florissant Valley Community College, continued the winning tradition at Saint Louis University, matching his predecessor's five NCAA championships. His successor at "Flo Valley," Coach Pete Sorber, won national titles at that level. Soon the Cougars of SIUE, boasting many stars from St. Louis parishes, became the Billikens' main rival. They faced each other five times in NCAA playoffs. The Cougars won the NCAA trophy twice. Ed Hueneke, a member of Our Lady of Good Counsel Parish, eventually took Guelker's place and followed in his winning ways. Both schools numbered many superb athletes.* Public high schools in the area failed to promote soccer. The sport was such a Catholic enclave that the mother of SLU's Gene Geimer used to tell her neighbors in the stands that her son was the only Lutheran ever on a Billiken team. It seemed appropriate that the director of the Archdiocesan Catholic Youth Organization, Monsignor Louis Meyer, had himself been a soccer star in his youth.

*See Appendix A, page 126.

Above: In a landmark sermon, on February 11, 1944, Father Claude Heithaus, S.J., brought before the students of Saint Louis University, and the entire local community, the moral and ethical issues involved in racial segregation.

✝ Chapter Twenty-Three
A Low-Key Midwesterner

Who would succeed Cardinal Glennon? Conversations among clergy suggested the old Irish-German divide. Priests, gathered for Forty Hours' Devotion at Our Lady of Perpetual Help Church, suggested Bishop Aloisius Muench of Fargo, North Dakota, soon to become a cardinal of the Church. A week later, another gathering of clergy, this one at Holy Name Parish boosted the candidacy of Bishop Edwin O'Hara of Kansas City, Missouri.

No one mentioned the name of Joseph Elmer Ritter, ceremoniously installed that summer as archbishop of Indianapolis. He had been named archbishop of his native Indiana several years before, but World War II had delayed the formal ceremony. In 1946 he faced two installations in one year. Pope Pius XII sent him 250 miles west on U.S. 40. He arrived in St. Louis without fanfare during the World Series between the Red Sox and the Cardinals.

Two writers for the *Globe-Democrat*, Martin Duggan and Justin Faherty, introduced the previously unknown midwesterner. In general, under the leadership of publisher G. Duncan Bauman, the *Globe-Democrat* supported the new archbishop's initiatives. Archbishop Ritter publicly thanked the *Globe* writers for their welcoming words. While he was St. Louis's first archbishop of German ancestry, most St. Louisans looked upon him as a fellow midwesterner.

The coming of St. Louis's first archbishop of German-American ancestry ironically ended the distinct story of the German Catholics of St. Louis. New loyalties grew: to the neighborhood where one lived or to the high school one attended. St. Louisans had no connection with the new Republic of West Germany, even though it included all of their ancestral provinces. As a result, from here on, this history will no longer concern itself with German-American organizations, but will single out individuals of German ancestry who significantly influenced the development of the city. Two individuals stand out: Joseph Elmer Ritter, archbishop of St. Louis, and Leonor Kretzer

Left: Cardinal Ritter meets with leaders of the Archdiocesan Council of Catholic Woman.

Sullivan, congresswoman from South St. Louis.

In his early months, the new archbishop kept a low profile. When Konrad Cardinal von Preysing of Berlin came to St. Louis to thank the people of the archdiocese for help immediately after the war, Archbishop Ritter invited Monsignor Charles Helmsing, a stately priest and a fluent pulpit orator, to welcome the distinguished guest at a solemn High Mass at the Cathedral. The new archbishop celebrated the Mass. He left preaching to the preachers.

A chance remark of Archbishop Ritter gave an indication of what his first significant move might be. When his driver pointed out St. Elizabeth's as a "black parish," the new archbishop demurred: "We have only Catholic parishes."

In the fall of 1947, Archbishop Ritter directed the schools of the archdiocese to accept all pupils living in the parish, regardless of race. Parishioners of a few parishes north of Forest Park took exception to Archbishop Ritter's call for recognition of the equality of all Catholics. Parishioners of other parishes of that area joined in the protest. But the Southside parishioners kept silent. Presuming that Missouri school law prohibited integration, the leader of the protesting parents threatened to go to court. In response, Archbishop Ritter simply called attention to the law of the Church that brought automatic excommunication upon a Catholic who called his own bishop into court for action in the line of duty. The protest leader, John Barrett, acquiesced and, to his credit, became an apostle of racial justice as a state senator.

In that one act, Archbishop Ritter won acclaim as one of the nation's leading social reformers. But he quietly rejected the praise, saying he was only doing his duty as a shepherd. He had not walked a picket line or organized a public protest. He simply had done what was right, as God required of him as shepherd.

Archbishop Ritter withdrew the archdiocese from the *Register* chain of newspapers published in Denver for St. Louis and most of the smaller western dioceses. The staff at the *Register* jokingly referred to its formula as: "Picture the bishop on the front

Right: Local St. Vincent de Paul Society President Robert Gronemeyer and his wife Mary (right) celebrate the society's 150th anniversary with national president and St. Louisan Joseph Mueller and his wife Nancy.

page, the bishop on the back, and any possible places between." Perhaps it was this identification of the diocese with its bishop that provoked this withdrawal. Monsignor Robert Stitz edited the new *St. Louis Review.*

Three new parishes opened every year, none with an ancestral designation. All were Catholic and American. Many of them on the Northside and in Northwest County stood on streets named for saints in subdivisions developed by the Vatterott Brothers. The archdiocese opened five new high schools, all co-educational. Only parish high schools, such as St. John the Baptist, had been co-educational before this time. Among noted educators in these schools were Sister Carl Mary Winkelmann, S.S.N.D., principal of Rosary, and Sister Lizette Bathe, R.S.M., principal of Mercy High.

Archbishop Ritter met regularly with lay leaders to discuss archdiocesan matters. One was a brilliant young historian with a large family and, at that time, no car. The archbishop picked him up on the way to the meetings. More and more people realized that an unusual archbishop had come among them.

The archbishop presided at the groundbreaking ceremonies for a library at Saint Louis University named for Pope Pius XII in 1957. The library would house microfilms of treasures of the Vatican Library. The Very Reverend Paul C. Reinert, S.J., was president of the university at the time and rector of the Jesuit Community. The chairman of the University President's Council, Dr. Carroll A. Hochwalt, vice president of Monsanto Chemical Company, urged a community drive for university expansion. Alvin Griesedieck chaired a committee in this drive. Archbishop Ritter gave his support. The university officials, in turn, named the Arts and Sciences Building Ritter Hall.

The archbishop became archiepiscopal moderator of the Sodality of Our Lady that had its Service Center at the Queen's Work Publishing House on South Grand, near Arsenal Street. The Sodality published the *Queen's Work* magazine for youth and sponsored summer leadership schools in various parts of the country. Father Daniel A. Lord, S.J., and others wrote pamphlets for general patronage. Jesuit Aloysius Heeg wrote catechisms for children that put the message of the *Baltimore Catechism* into the language of third graders. Alice Schatzman assisted him. Dorothy Willmann promoted Sodalities for women, along with Bessie Kull and Doris Schoenhoff.

Ligouri Publications, under the direction of Father Don Miller, C.SS.R., expanded from the publication of a successful magazine, the *Ligourian*, to religious pamphlets that sold on racks in the vestibules of countless churches, and later added soft-cover books. When the Jesuits closed the Queen's Work Publishing Center, the Redemptorists took over the many titles made popular by Father Lord and other writers, thus expanding the staff of pamphleteers beyond Redemptorist writers.

Among the priests of the archdiocese who rose to the episcopacy at that time, Father Leo J. Steck, pastor of St. Gabriel's Church, accepted a call to be auxiliary of Salt Lake City. Monsignor Charles Helmsing became bishop of a newly created diocese of Springfield–Cape Girardeau, and later head of the Kansas City, Missouri, diocese. Fathers George Gottwald and Charles Koester became auxiliary bishops of St. Louis. At this time also, local religious superiors rose to higher positions. Father Sylvester P. Juergens, provincial of the St. Louis Province of the Marianists since 1936, was elected superior general of the congregation at the General Chapter in 1946. The first American to hold this position, he established five new provinces and two missions. At the conclusion of his term in 1956, he returned to Chaminade College in St. Louis County and engaged in a varied ministry. Father Paul C. Reinert, S.J., president of Saint Louis University and rector of the Jesuit community from 1949 to 1968, became president of the Jesuit Educational Association. Reinert gave up his position as rector of the Jesuit community, but he remained as university president. Up to that time, Jesuit priests on the university faculty made up the Board of Trustees of the university. A president's council of laymen, chaired at first by Dr. Hochwalt, had exercised only an advisory function. Now a board composed of laymen and Jesuit priests from around the country guided Saint Louis University. Reinert invited Daniel L. Schlafly, a Georgetown graduate and member of the St. Louis Public School Board, to head the new Board of Trustees.

Dr. Hochwalt, as well as many other St. Louisans of Germanic ancestry, chaired the annual Archdiocesan Development Appeal. Among them were the already mentioned Richard C. Muckerman and the Vatterott brothers, Joseph and Charles, Jr. Others were Cornelius Weilbacher, Captain Joseph Streckfus, Harry F. Bussmann, Henry J. Elmendorf, and C. Kaemmerlen, during the Ritter years. Hochwalt later accepted the chairmanship of the Board of Trustees of the Catholic University of America.

Many individuals were in the news. Among them, the Reverend John C. Miller, C.S.C., who directed the Central Bureau at 3835 Westminster Place, now a center for research with its extensive collection of German-American historical material. Mae Mosher Duggan headed the Citizens for Educational Freedom. Service units honored Colonel Lee Meyer, a teacher in peacetime, the ranking woman officer in the area. Jack Zehrt won acclaim for excellent photography, especially his photograph of the Glider accident that killed Mayor Dee Becker. The Reverend William F. Schwienher guided programming on the Sacred Heart Program, which was carried weekly by a thousand stations throughout the country. Robert Gronemeyer headed the local unit of the St. Vincent de Paul Society.

From its outset, St. Louis had been a missionary diocese. Further, St. Louisans contributed to the missions far out of proportion to their numbers, according to Monsignor (later Bishop) Charles Helmsing, director of the National Office of the Society for the Propagation of the Faith. Religious orders from St. Louis had continued to send missionaries to the Sioux and Arapahoe in the West, to Belize and Honduras in Central America, and to Africa.* The archdiocese began its own mission effort in La Paz, Bolivia. Father Andrew Schierhoff became auxiliary bishop there.

According to Roman rumors, the archdiocesan missionary venture in Bolivia played a part in the naming of Archbishop Ritter as a cardinal of the Church by Pope John XXIII in 1961. The other new cardinal at the consistory also had a connection with the Church in Latin America. The rumor may have reflected the facts.

In his early years in St. Louis, Archbishop Ritter frowned on inter-faith discussion but strongly urged inter-denominational community cooperation. In one instance, he supported a Jewish congregation in an effort to locate a synagogue in a particular neighborhood. Later he fostered inter-faith discussions.

At the second Vatican Council, Archbishop Ritter made his presence felt early in the first session. He urged the fathers to reject a document on scripture and tradition that failed to recognize twentieth-century biblical studies. His straightforward words had their part in updating attitudes, in line with the earlier encyclical of Pope Pius XII on scriptural studies, *Divino afflante Spiritu*, of 1944.

While the story of Cardinal Ritter at the Council calls for a lengthy treatise in itself, these were the highlights. He became a vocal force in discussions on the missions, ecumenism, Jewish-Christian relationships, and religious liberty. He was on the prevailing side in all these issues. Pope John XXIII's fresh views prevailed.

Archbishop Ritter never lost his unsophisticated midwestern ways. On one occasion, between sessions of the Council, he invited a prominent Swiss theologian to speak at a gathering of churchmen at Kenrick Seminary. When called to speak, the visitor asked: "Isn't the great cardinal of the West coming?" Presumably, he anticipated a formal entry by the cardinal with a blare of trumpets.

"That's the cardinal in the second row, talking to a Lutheran minister," said the chairman of the meeting. Before the visiting theologian left the country, he ranked this experience among his two most delightful memories of America.

Cardinal Ritter died on June 10, 1967, shortly after the formal closing of the Council. A mosaic on the East Wall of the Historic Bay in the great Cathedral on Lindell recalls his work in ecumenism and racial justice. A high school in mid-town and a building at Saint Louis University bear his name.

---

*See also Appendix B, page 127.

Chapter Twenty-Four
Leonor Kretzer Sullivan:
Consumers' Advocate

During the years that Cardinal Ritter guided the religious life of the people of St. Louis, their most significant political figure of German-Catholic ancestry was Congresswoman Leonor Kretzer Sullivan of the Third District of Missouri, the first woman to represent Missouri in the House of Representatives. She grew up in southwest St. Louis, the daughter of Frederick W. Kretzer, who had a tailoring establishment on Lafayette Avenue. Her mother was Nora Nostrand, a woman remembered by her neighbors as one "who dressed up even to go to the corner grocery."

Leonor attended public and private schools and took night courses at Washington University. She sang in the St. Aloysius parish choir. She taught business arithmetic and accounting and served as placement director of the St. Louis Comptrometer School. In 1941 she joined the League of Women Voters. On December 27 of that same year she married John Berchmans Sullivan at St. Aloysius Church. A lawyer who had served as secretary to the mayor and had been active in Democratic politics, Sullivan had just won a seat in the 77th Congress from the Third District of Missouri.

Mrs. Sullivan served as an aide to her husband during the 77th and 78th Congress, from 1941 until 1947, and then in the 81st and 82nd from January 1949 until his death two years later. Mrs. Sullivan remained in Washington as secretary to Congressman Theodore Leonard Irving of Kansas City. She ran for the seat of her late husband in January 1953, and the Southside voters elected her to the 83rd Congress. They re-elected her for eleven more terms, until 1977, when she declined to run for the 95th Congress.

During this time she became known for her support of consumer rights, especially in product labeling and meat inspection. In the 1950s, she waged a five-year battle to win approval for a plan that finally became law in 1959, to distribute government surplus foods to the needy. She was the principal author of the 1968 Credit Protection

Act. No doubt, the memory of her husband played a great part in her original election, but over the years she established herself much more strongly in the memory of people as a consumers' advocate.

A lifelong fan of the Mississippi River, Sullivan promoted the St. Louis Port flood control projects and river safety bills. She was also a driving force behind legislation that supported construction of the Jefferson National Expansion Memorial, the famous Gateway Arch, on the riverfront. She was not satisfied with the erection of the Arch but continued her interest. When the Arch museum shop, for instance, neglected to feature the book of excellent photographs of the Arch by Robert Arteaga, Mrs. Sullivan saw that it became available to visitors. When architect Ted Wofford released his feasibility study of St. Joseph's Shrine on the near Northside, she supported the successful drive to preserve the historic church.

In 1983 St. Louis honored her by refurbishing Wharf Street and renaming it "Leonor K. Sullivan Boulevard."

Right: Congresswoman
Leonor Kretzer Sullivan.

✠ Chapter Twenty-Five
Approaching the Third Millenium

After World War I, American public opinion scorned the notion of hyphenated-Americans. Everyone was to be 100 percent American and to forego ancestral customs. That attitude lasted half a century. Then "Black became beautiful," the Irish began annual St. Patrick's Day parades, the Italians welcomed neighbors to "Hill Day," and Mexican nationals celebrated *Cinquo de Maio*, the Fifth of May, their independence day.

In the 1970s, German Americans began a series of annual Strassenfests on the streets in downtown St. Louis during the summer. These enjoyable weekends had no religious connection or significance, but individual Catholics such as Herman Eisele of Resurrection Parish served on the board of directors. Each year a representative of Stuttgart, St. Louis' sister city, came as an honored guest. On one occasion, the mayor of Stuttgart, son of the legendary "Desert Fox," General Erwin Rommel of World War II, represented his city.

The German Cultural Society opened a welcoming center on Grand Boulevard at Winnebago Street for refugees from Communist persecution. These Germans had not lived in the Fatherland, but in various places in the Balkans. While this organization was not solely for and of Catholics, it reflected the spirit of the German-Catholic community that had always welcomed immigrants.

German restaurants again flourished: Herman and Theresa Eisele's Bavarian Inn on Arsenal Street near Gravois Avenue and the new Black Forest on Cherokee Street at Michigan Avenue in South St. Louis, Schneithorst's Hoffamberg Inn on Lindbergh Boulevard near Clayton Avenue in West County, and Hendels across from Sacred Heart Church in Florissant.

Changing neighborhoods and public housing programs forced many changes in the old traditional German-language parishes. St. Liborius closed as a parish church but continued as a neighborhood center. St. Henry's was used by a Protestant congre-

Above: Traditional German dancing sponsored by the German Cultural Society.

gation until fire destroyed it. St. Augustine's became a Protestant church. St. Bernard's felt the "headache ball." Holy Ghost joined with Visitation, originally an Irish parish. St. Agatha's Church welcomed ultraconservative Catholics by offering worship in Latin according to the pre-Vatican II rite. St. Mary's of the Victories, the oldest German church in the city, became a place of devotion for Hungarian immigrants. It bore the name St. Stephen's for a time. Later, the name St. Mary's was restored.

After a decline for some time, the congregation of Sts. Peter and Paul regrouped, with a community renewal in the Soulard area. Housing projects developed there that strengthened the parish, as they did St. Vincent de Paul, a multinational parish where many German American immigrants had worshiped.

An energetic group of citizens of all national backgrounds and of various religious traditions formed "The Friends of St. Joseph" to save the old church from the headache ball. The head of the archdiocesan Office of Buildings had talked of demolition. The Friends won out. St. Joseph's is now a shrine, the only baroque church in St. Louis. Father Valentine, O.F.M. Cap., directs it.

After Vatican II and the death of Cardinal Ritter, Bishop John J. Carberry of Columbus, Ohio, a native of Brooklyn, New York, became bishop of St. Louis. In that period of post-Vatican II adjustment, the archbishop reflected the conservative views of the eastern seaboard. He soon became a cardinal.

Two Catholic organizations that had given generous service to the public in the United States and had a strong connection with St. Louis celebrated anniversaries in the last quarter of the century, the Catholic Knights of America and the St. Vincent de Paul Society. While the Knights began in Nashville, Tennessee, among a group of Irish immigrants, many German parishes in St. Louis fostered branches. The Cathedral on the waterfront hosted the Knights on their 100th anniversary on Sunday, April 24, 1977. To carry on the spiritual uplift of the anniversary, the spiritual director, Monsignor Vincent Naes, pastor of St. Cecilia's Church, who had published a history of the first hundred years of achievement called *Rounding Out a Century*, wrote a book of meditations, *Lift Up Your Heart*.

In 1980 Bishop John L. May of Mobile succeeded Cardinal Carberry. May was a native of Chicago of Alsatian ancestry. His frank and open approach appealed to the people of St. Louis. In one of his early actions, he responded to ultraconservative people who protested Saint Louis University's invitation to a controversial theologian of Catholic University. "A university," Archbishop May responded, "should be a place where controversial questions are discussed." That ended the complaints but not the discussion.

The archbishop took steps that might have been taken years before. He started a program called Renew, under the general supervision of Father John J. Hughes and the executive direction of pastor Father William Scheid and Mary Ann Klohr, a school principal. The Renew program called for discussion and implementation of the decrees of Vatican II. The program was well received by the people of St. Louis. The only complaint was that it should have come sooner after the Vatican Council.

Individual Catholics of German ancestry continued to achieve. Among the clergy, Fathers John Leibricht became bishop of South Missouri, John Wurm bishop of Belleville, and Paul Zipfel bishop of Bismarck, North Dakota. Among lay people, the Vatterott brothers, Charles and Joe, adorned North County with more streets named for saints in the developments that they undertook. In an area just west of Lindbergh, for instance, that had originally been part of the St. Stanislaus Seminary property, they named all the streets after Jesuit saints. One could buy a ranch-type house on Gonzaga Lane, or Kostka, or Borgia, even if one's patron saint was St. Francis or St. Dominic. Joseph Vatterott, a member of the Board of Trustees of Saint Louis University, blocked the threatened alienation of Parks College of Aeronautical Technology. In spite of the college's historic connection with all the pioneers of flight, the university administrators seemed willing to let the school drift in the Cahokia bottomlands. Vatterott shared the widespread hope that it remain an integral part of Saint Louis University.

Father Claude Heithaus, S.J., who had earlier gained fame as a promoter of racial justice, developed the finest museum of religious history in the Midwest in the old Rock Building at St. Stanislaus Seminary in northwest St. Louis County. It gained the name Museum of the Western Jesuit Missions. His brother William set up the St. Stanislaus Historical Museum Society, a nonprofit organization of the state of Missouri, to help promote the museum. He gave his entire estate to this purpose.

Individuals of German ancestry still continued to be "joiners," but the organizations that they joined were not exclusively German. Charles Finniger headed the "Friends of St. Joseph Shrine" in their successful drive to save the historic church. Rose Ann Fanz and Dave Eschman were co-presidents for ten years of the St. Louis Corral of the Westerners, a society of amateur historians interested in the story of the American West. John and Jane Finklang and Andy Fanz were long-standing members. Mary Jo and John Nischwitz belonged to the Civil War Roundtable. Bob Bieg, Bill Olwig, and Dan Venverloh were active in the Laymen's Retreat League. Ray Mohrman and Joe Gross served with Serra International. John Herbers, Tim Hessel, and Andy Bosch held long-time memberships in the Manresa Society. Mary Ann Kramer Wuller, Jeanne Frett, Janet Knobbe, and Les and Connie Kappel skated with the Winter Garden Club. Bob and Marcella Garger and Joe and Audrey Heidenry had permanent memberships in the Tower Grove Tennis Club. Bern Nordman and Hilbert Weber were active St. Louis University High School alumni, and John Krey Stevens, Bill Kessler, Roy Gillyon, alumni, and the Koop sisters, Barbara Lynch, Judy McGraugh, and Gretchen Schulze, alumnae of Saint Louis University. Sisters Marylu Stueber, Dionysia Brockland, and Virginia Volkerding were among the charter members of the St. Louis Area Religious Archivists.

The German community joined in the welcome for Archbishop Justin Rigali, who succeeded Archbishop May upon his resignation. During one of the new archbishop's early years in St. Louis, fire swept the roof of St. Anthony's Church, a landmark for the Southside German community for a century and a quarter. Archbishop Rigali supported the decision of the pastor, Father Francis Coens, O.F.M., to refurbish the edifice, St. Louisans of all ancestries and beliefs rejoiced.

The Society of St. Vincent de Paul celebrated 150 years of its foundation in St. Louis in 1995. A booklet, *The Society of St. Vincent de Paul: 150 Years of Service in the United States*, memorialized the occasion. German Americans had been part of the original group that met in St. Louis and started the first unit of the Society in America. Father Ambrose G. Heim was spiritual director, and Dr. L. B. Ganahl and Senator H. J. Spaunhorst were charter members. German Americans continued in this good work. The national president, on the occasion of the 150th anniversary in 1995, was Joseph Mueller, and the St. Louis council president was Robert Gronemeyer, both men of Germanic ancestry.

To close the century with jubilation, Pope John Paul II visited St. Louis in the last year of the old millenium. As all St. Louisans, those of German ancestry moved into the new millenium with confidence and courage, and gratification that they had helped make St. Louis one of the greatest archdioceses in the world and a place where all people could find a home.

 *Epilogue*

"The farther one moves west and north in Germany, the stronger the Catholicism." With these words, Jesuit historian Father Raymond Corrigan began his favorite talk on the Church in nineteenth-century Europe. Head of the history department at Saint Louis University in the 1930s, he had just completed his doctorate at the University of Munich in Bavaria and spoke with authority on the subject.

These northwestern provinces were the Rhineland, Hanover, and Westphalia, especially the diocese of Paderborn. Most of the St. Louis Germans came from these areas. A few came from Bavaria in the South. Immigrants came in great numbers during the time of Archbishop Peter Richard Kenrick (1843–1895).

The archbishop encouraged immigrants and wrote to archbishops in Europe: "St. Louis is the most Catholic city in the country and in many ways reflects the true spirit of Catholicism." The archbishop had a strong hand in welcoming German immigrants. He followed the principle of gradual Americanization. He allowed sermons and religious instructions in the language of the Old Country, unlike other archbishops who wanted immediate Americanization. That would develop gradually in St. Louis.

The new-coming Germans deeply appreciated this. Father Francis Goller, popular pastor of Sts. Peter and Paul, singled out Archbishop Kenrick at the Archbishop's episcopal jubilee as "The Father of the Immigrant."

The coming of German and Irish Catholics to St. Louis in relatively similar numbers in the middle decades of the nineteenth century gave the Church in St. Louis a more solid base than most American cities. New York, Philadelphia, and Boston had exclusively Irish leadership during those years. Chicago, San Francisco, Los Angeles, and Miami were small places then. St. Louis had Irish archbishops from 1843 to 1946. But vicar-generals of German ancestry gave a counter-balancing, and at one time they were the spiritual leaders of German Catholics everywhere.

Many German-speaking priests had studied beyond the boundaries of their native land, in Italy, in Belgium, or in Austria, and handled various languages. Irish priests usually were familiar only with English. This gave them an entree into American life, but it allowed them less opportunity to help newcomers from Italy or Bohemia.

Next, the coming of the Germans added a sense of stability and conservatism. They brought knowledge of the liturgy and prepared their people for needed changes in worship.

Archbishop Kenrick's policy of gradual Americanization allowed the non-English–speaking immigrants to establish themselves gradually in American life. The German immigrants deeply appreciated this principle and in gratitude offered their resources and talents to develop parishes where they came to feel at home. And they stayed, and all St. Louisans gladly felt their presence.

Appendix A
St. Louis Collegiate Soccer Stars

Among All-Americans of Saint Louis University, Jack Dueker, Al Trost, Bill Vieth, and Wally Werner were first team choices, and Steve Frank, Joe Hamm, Jerry Knobbe, John Klein, and Tom Trost merited second team. The trophy for the most valuable player in the NCAA went to Jack Dueker in 1959, to Don Range in 1960, to John Klein in 1961, and to Al Trost in both 1969 and 1970. Mike Sorber, son of Coach Pete Sorber at "Flo Valley," played on the World Cup team. Other notable Billikens were Dave Kuenzle, Jim Tjetjens, John Eilermann, Joe Westhus, Ed Neusel, Dave Schlitt, Mark Frederickson, Bruce Rudroff, Larry Hulcer, Don Huber, Frank Schuler, Don Droege, Jim and Tom Bokern, Bob Matteson, Steve Rick, Mark Demling, Jim Draude, Denny Werner, Jim and Joe Leeker, and others.

Edwardsville stars from St. Louis included, among others, Ed and Denny Huneke, Tom Groak, Jim Nitz, Leo Stremlau, Larry and Steve Schmidt, Jim Guelker (the coach's son), Jim Hoff, Jim Kersting, Don Ebert, and All-Americans John Stremlau and Bob Kessen. Ed Huneke eventually succeeded Bob Guelker as coach. Denny Vanniger starred at St. Mary's High and Harris-Stowe College.

Many St. Louis young men went to other colleges and universities, among them Rich Nelke and Guy Bush at Michigan State, Matt Sauer at Quincy College, and others at Navy, Rockhurst, Stetson, and South Florida. Ray Schnettgoecke went to Brown, where he won all-Ivy League honors before playing in the professional league. He won a headline on a Philadelphia sports page: "Ray What's His Name? Scored Three Times."

Above: SLU NCAA soccer stars.

✟ Appendix B
St. Louis Missionaries in Africa

The missionary record of the archdiocese took a new step after Vatican II, a step to Africa. Among the dedicated St. Louisans who went on the mission to Africa, two deserve special mention, Sister Mary Lorenz Blatz, S.S.N.D., and Sister Shirley Kolmer, A.S.C. Sister Lorenz attended Sts. Peter and Paul School. She entered the novitiate of the School Sisters of Notre Dame and took her vows in 1935. She earned a bachelor's and a master's degree, majoring in geography.

Over a period of forty years she taught on the elementary level in Illinois and Missouri, and at some of these schools she held the principal's post also. The Phi Delta Kappa sorority gave her its Distinguished Service Award for her contribution to educational administration. Missioned next to Port Loko, Sierra Leone, Sister Lorenz taught at a Women's Teachers' College and worked with the disadvantaged. The people of Port Loko named a street after her. In her next assignment she directed an adult education program among the Papago in Arizona.

Sister Shirley Kolmer, A.S.C., missionary and martyr, was born December 15, 1930, on the rich prairie near Waterloo, Illinois, thirty miles southeast of the St. Louis metropolitan area. She attended Catholic elementary school in Waterloo and high school at the motherhouse of the Sisters Adorers of the Precious Blood at Ruma, six miles further south. She entered the motherhouse and made her religious profession July 1, 1947. She dedicated her life to education, first as a grade school teacher, then as a high school teacher, and finally as a professor of mathematics at Saint Louis University. She also served as formation director of the order, as a member of the provincial council, and as provincial superior.

In 1977, she went to Liberia, West Africa, as a Fulbright professor of mathematics at the University of Liberia in the capital, Monrovia, for a year. During the next five years she served as provincial superior at Ruma, returning to Liberia in January 1984. There she again taught at the university. She then became the principal of a diocesan high school. She set out to establish a teachers' training center to improve the quality of teaching in the country. Her death, along with that of four other members of her sisterhood, at the hands of the rebels during the Civil War in October 1992, cut short that longed-for goal.

Sculptor Rudi Torini erected a statue to the memory of the martyred nuns on the grounds of the motherhouse in Ruma.

Left: Sister Mary Lorenz Blatz.
Right: Sculpture by Rudi Torini.

 *End Notes*

Preface

1   J. Thomas Scharf, *History of St. Louis City and County*, Philadelphia, 1883, p. 1640.
2   Catholic Baptisms, St. Louis Missouri, 1765–1840, published by the St. Louis Genealogical Society in 1982.
3   Bishop Du Bourg's Account Book in St. Louis Archdiocesan Archives (hereafter SLAA). See also Paul C. Schulte, *The Catholic History of St. Louis,* St. Louis, 1934.

1   Early German-Catholic Immigrants

1   U.S. Bureau of Census, 1840, p. 321.

2   Cathedral on the Riverfront

1   Fenwick to Rosati, Nov. 6, 1837, in SLAA.
2   *Catholic Almanac for 1839.* Baltimore, pp. 114–116.
3   p. 125
4   p. 122
5   p. 107
6   p. 102
7   p. 69
8   Olson, Audrey L., S.L., *St. Louis Germans, 1850–1920*, New York, Arno Press, 1980, p. 307, n. 3.

3   Archbishop Kenrick Welcomes More German Catholics

1   Kenrick to Milde, Nov. 9, 1843, in SLAA.
2   Kenrick to Milde, Aug. 29, 1844, in SLAA.

3   Kenrick to Milde, Dec. 10, 1844, in SLAA.

4   *Ibid.*

5   The Coming of Germans of Other Faiths

1   Scharf, p. 202.

2   Audrey Olson, p. 124.

6   More German-Catholic Parishes Open

1   Seventh Census, Statistics of Missouri, Table II, 552, Manuscript Census
     Enumeration, 1850.

2   John Rothensteiner, *History of the Archdiocese of St. Louis*, St. Louis, 1928,
     Vol. I., p. 153.

8   Irish and German Catholics

1   Kenrick, St. Louis, to Purcell, May 2, 1858, in the library at the University of
     Notre Dame.

9   German Catholics and the Civil War

1   *Catholic Almanac*, 1864.

10   New Churches

1   Rothensteiner, II, 1853.

2   A. Barhaus, S.J., *A Short Historical Sketch of the German Catholic Congregation
     of the Sacred Heart of Jesus at Florissant, Mo.*, 1883, pp. 5 ff.

14   Problems And Progress

1   William Linz, Herder and Co., *The New Catholic Encyclopedia*, Vol. 5, p. 766.

15   Catholics in Controversy

1   Gerald P. Fogarty, S.J., *Denis J. O'Connell: Americanist Agent at the Vatican*, New
     Haven, 1969, p. 61.

2   *Westliche Post*, June 21, 1891.

3   *Associated Press*, June 13, 1891.

4   *New York Herald*, December 13, 1892.

5   John Conway, "Cahenslyism versus Americanism," in the *Review of Reviews*
     (6, No. 32, August 1892, p. 45).

16   German-Catholic Press

1   Philip Gleason, *The Conservative Reformer*, German Catholics and the Social Order,
     Notre Dame, 1968, p. 101.

2   *Ibid.*, p. 121.

3   Olson, pp. 117.

17 Architects and Masters of Art Glass
1   Annemarie Springer, *Nineteenth Century German-American Church Artists*, p. 367

18 Trenches in France, Retrenchment in St. Louis
1   *The Great Silent Minority: Missouri's Resistance to WWI,* Columbia, 1988, *passim.*
2   *Post-Dispatch*, July 15, 1918.
3   *Ibid.*, June 10, 1918.
4   Olson, pp. 118, 210.
5   *The St. Louis Star*, Oct. 10, 1921.

19 Troubled Twenties
1   Gleason, 105.
2   Joseph Matt, "Frederick P. Kenkel: An Evaluation of the Man," in *Social Justice Review*, Vol. 81 (Feb. 1990), No. 2, p. 40.
3   Gleason, p. 189.
4   Gleason, p. 206.
5   Thomas T. McEvoy, C.S.C., *A History of the Catholic Church in the United States*, University of Notre Dame Press, 1969, p. 399.
6   *The Catholic Encyclopedia, passim.*
7   John Rothensteiner, "On the Writing of Parish Histories," in *Fortnightly Review*, September 15, 1916.
8   Stephen A. Werner, *Prophet of the Christian Social Manifesto: Joseph Husslein, S.J.: His Life, Work, and Social Thought*, Milwaukee, Marquette University Press, 2001.

 *Index*

✝ About the Author

Over the past forty years, Father William Barnaby Faherty, S.J., has received invitations to write the story of the most important botanical garden in the world and its founder, Henry Shaw; of the most influential flight school and its chief, Oliver Lafayette Parks; of space exploration at NASA's installation in Florida; of the St. Louis archdiocese; and of the city itself. *The Concise History of St. Louis*, co-authored with neighborhood specialist NiNi Harris, has recently come out in its fourth edition.

Following the advice of one of his mentors, Pulitzer Prize–winner Paul Horgan, Faherty tried his hand several times with fiction. MGM adapted his first novel, *A Wall for San Sebastian*, for a movie. His third novel *The Call of Pope Octavian* tells of a future pope who updates the administrative machinery of the Papacy as Vatican II has updated external attitudes. The Missouri Writers' Guild has rated several of his books the best work of the year.

His *St. Louis Irish: An Unmatched Celtic Community* went into its fourth printing and brought many requests for a companion book on the German Catholics.

A native of St. Louis of Irish-Alsatian ancestry, Father Faherty received a Doctor of Philosophy degree in History at Saint Louis University in 1949. Rockhurst University conferred on him an honorary Doctorate in Humane Letters in 1993.